How to Read World Literature

How to Study Literature

The books in this series – all written by eminent scholars renowned for their teaching abilities – show students how to read, understand, write, and criticize literature. They provide the key skills which every student of literature must master, as well as offering a comprehensive introduction to the field itself.

Published

How to Study Theory	Wolfgang Iser
How to Write a Poem	John Redmond
How to Read a Shakespeare Play	David Bevington
How to Read the Victorian Novel	George Levine
How to Read World Literature	David Damrosch

How to Read
World Literature

David Damrosch

WILEY-BLACKWELL

A John Wiley & Sons, Ltd., Publication

This edition first published 2009
© 2009 David Damrosch

Blackwell Publishing was acquired by John Wiley & Sons in February 2007.
Blackwell's publishing program has been merged with Wiley's global Scientific,
Technical, and Medical business to form Wiley-Blackwell.

Registered Office
John Wiley & Sons Ltd, The Atrium, Southern Gate, Chichester, West Sussex,
PO19 8SQ, United Kingdom

Editorial Offices
350 Main Street, Malden, MA 02148-5020, USA
9600 Garsington Road, Oxford, OX4 2DQ, UK
The Atrium, Southern Gate, Chichester, West Sussex, PO19 8SQ, UK

For details of our global editorial offices, for customer services, and for information
about how to apply for permission to reuse the copyright material in this book please
see our website at www.wiley.com/wiley-blackwell.

Library of Congress Cataloging-in-Publication Data

Damrosch, David.
  How to read world literature / David Damrosch.
    p. cm.—(How to study literature)
  Includes bibliographical references and index.
  ISBN 978-1-4051-6826-7 (pbk. : alk. paper)—ISBN 978-1-4051-6827-4
(hardcover : alk. paper) 1. Literature—History and criticism. I. Title.

  PN524.D36 2009
  809—dc22

                                                    2008013066

A catalogue record for this title is available from the British Library.

Set in 10.5/13pt Minion by Graphicraft Limited, Hong Kong
Printed and bound in Singapore by Utopia Press Pte Ltd

1 2009

To my students

Contents

Acknowledgments

Teaching at Columbia University over the past quarter-century has not only given me the opportunity to refine ideas on reading world literature; it has brought the world into my classrooms. Just this past semester, a seminar on border-crossings and double identities included students from Australia, Croatia, Egypt, Finland, France, Israel, Italy, and Poland. This book is dedicated to Columbia's lively, argumentative, insatiably curious students, who have taught me at least as much as I've taught them.

These pages have gained much from the conversation in seminars co-taught with Wiebke Denecke, Orhan Pamuk, Sheldon Pollock, and Pauline Yu. I owe much as well to less formal conversations with colleagues at Columbia and elsewhere, including Emily Apter, Sandra Bermann, David Kastan, Pericles Lewis, Stephen Owen, Elizabeth Richmond-Garza, Haun Saussy, and Gayatri Spivak, and to the extended process of work on *The Longman Anthology of World Literature* with my friends April Alliston, Marshall Brown, Page duBois, Sabry Hafez, Ursula Heise, Djelal Kadir, David Pike, Sheldon Pollock, Bruce Robbins, Haruo Shirane, Jane Tylus, and Pauline Yu.

The impetus for this book came from Emma Bennett, who has offered valuable guidance throughout, admirably seconded by Louise Butler and Hannah Morrell. I have benefited as well from generous and insightful readings by Wiebke Denecke, Valerie Henitiuk, and Martin Puchner, and from the loving support of my wife, Lori Fisler Damrosch. Clearly, it takes a world to write a book on world literature.

Introduction

Reaching back over nearly five millennia and extending today to almost every inhabited region of the globe, world literature offers its readers an unparalleled variety of literary pleasures and cultural experiences. Yet this very variety also poses exceptional challenges, as we cannot expect to approach all these works with the fund of cultural knowledge that readers share with writers within a single tradition. A reader of Balzac will come to know a good deal about Paris even without visiting the city, and as a result can better visualize scenes in Baudelaire and Proust; similarly, a good knowledge of the Qur'an is a prerequisite for a full appreciation of Arabic poetry. It can take many years to develop a close familiarity with even one culture; how are we to deal with the multitude of the world's literary cultures?

Apart from general context, literary traditions themselves are often highly culture-specific: the plays of Bernard Shaw and Tom Stoppard insistently recall Shakespeare, while the medieval Japanese *Tale of Genji* is filled with references to earlier Chinese and Japanese poetry, and modern Japanese novelists keep referring back to *Genji* in turn. Along with differing literary references, cultures develop distinctive assumptions about the ways literature should be created and understood. If we read a foreign text in ignorance of its author's assumptions and values, we risk reducing it to a pallid version of some literary form we already know, as though Homer had really wanted to write novels but couldn't quite handle character development, or as though Japanese haiku are would-be sonnets that run out of steam after seventeen syllables.

What is a non-specialist reader to do? If we don't want to confine our reading within the narrow compass of one or two of the world's literatures,

1

we need to develop ways to make the most of works from a range of distant times and places. This book is intended to meet this need, offering a set of modes of entry into the many worlds of world literature. The book's chapters highlight key issues that we encounter in confronting foreign material, showcasing conjunctions of major works that can exemplify fruitful approaches to reading world literature in the undergraduate classroom and beyond.

The challenges we face in dealing with the world's many literatures are very real, but I have written this book in the conviction that a work of world literature has an exceptional ability to transcend the boundaries of the culture that produces it. Certainly some works are so culture-bound that they can only be meaningful to a home-grown audience or to specialists in the area, and those texts remain within the realm of their original national or regional culture. Yet very many works find readers in distant times and places, speaking to us with compelling immediacy. No literary culture is more distant from us today, for instance, than the court of King Shulgi of Ur, the world's first known patron of literature, who reigned in southern Mesopotamia four thousand years ago. His very language, Sumerian, is unrelated to any other known language. It had already ceased to be spoken a thousand years before Homer, and its cuneiform script was unreadable for a full two thousand years until the late nineteenth century. Yet now that modern scholars have painstakingly deciphered the ancient language, no specialized knowledge whatever is required for us to respond to the charm of a lullaby written for one of Shulgi's sons:

> Sleep come, sleep come,
> sleep come to my son,
> sleep hasten to my son!
> Put to sleep his open eyes,
> settle your hand upon his sparkling eyes –
> as for his murmuring tongue,
> let the murmuring not spoil his sleep.
> ("Šulgi N," lines 12–18)

A great work of literature can often reach out beyond its own time and place, but conversely it can also provide a privileged mode of access into some of the deepest qualities of its culture of origin. Works of art refract their cultures rather than simply reflecting them, and even the most "realistic" painting or story is a stylized and selective representation. Even so, a great deal is conveyed through literature's kaleidoscopes and convex mirrors, and our appreciation of a work can be enormously increased if we learn more about the things it refers to and the artist's and audience's assumptions.

This is already the case for music and visual art, and it is all the more true for verbal creations, which recode so much in differing languages: Japanese and English people don't see different colors, but they do have different names for colors, some of them even dividing up the spectrum differently. We can learn much about a culture from its art and its architecture, but we learn immeasurably more when we have written records as well. If we read more of the poems King Shulgi commissioned, we soon find ourselves surrounded with an entire pantheon of unfamiliar gods and goddesses and a plethora of historical and literary allusions. Shulgi's poems give us an important mode of access to his culture, and that cultural knowledge helps us appreciate the poems in turn.

Reading a work from a distant time or place involves a back-and-forth movement between the familiar and the unfamiliar. A view of the world is always a view from wherever the observer is standing, and we inevitably filter what we read through our experience of what we have read in the past. But then, if we don't simply overlay our prior expectations wholesale onto the new work, its distinctive qualities will impress themselves on us, enlarging our field of vision and giving us a new purchase on the things we knew before.

World literature may seem daunting in its sheer scope, but this is already an issue with any major national tradition. More novels were written in nineteenth-century England than any single person could read in an entire lifetime. There is always more to read, but we can only read onward if we have gotten successfully oriented, at least in a preliminary way, by the very first works we have read. Reading our way beyond our home tradition involves a more pronounced version of the part–whole dilemma or hermeneutic circle that we already encounter in a single tradition. We have to start somewhere and work outward to a broader view. We will better understand what Dickens was doing if we have a deep knowledge of Defoe, Fielding, Jane Austen, Walter Scott, Trollope, and George Eliot, and our understanding will be further enlarged if we can view Dickens comparatively in relation to Diderot, Hugo, Goethe, Gogol, and Dostoevsky. Further, our sense of classic narratives is also shaped by the books now being written around us, and so we read Dickens in part through lenses provided by A. S. Byatt, Salman Rushdie, Peter Carey, and a host of other contemporary novelists.

relating to translation

3

A wide and deep familiarity with novels is wonderfully helpful for the appreciation of Dickens in England or of the Nigerian Chinua Achebe or Japan's Yukio Mishima, but we can never achieve such familiarity unless we can make some real sense of the first novel we read, and then the second one, and on though the tenth and the hundredth. This hermeneutical process can begin into childhood with the works that circulate in our home tradition, including books that have taken root as imports. The Bible and the *Thousand and One Nights* may have been known from such an early age that their very foreignness may seem comfortably familiar. If we now start to read beyond the boundaries of already familiar texts, we experience the shock of the new, but we can respond by bringing to bear the skills we developed when we first began to read.

This book is organized around a set of skills that we need to develop – or recover and hone – in order to read world literature with understanding and enjoyment. We need to become aware of different literary assumptions made in different cultures, including assumptions as to what is literature itself – its modes of creation and reading, its social setting and effects. This is the subject of the first chapter, which draws its examples chiefly from lyric poetry. The second chapter treats the issue of reading across time, using the Western epic tradition as a case in point: how do we come to terms with an older work's distinctive methods and worldview, and how do we assess its afterlife in the later tradition it helped to shape? Building on the first two chapters, the third chapter turns to the problem of reading across cultures, now with case studies drawn from drama.

The fourth chapter discusses the fascinating problems raised when we read in translation, as readers of world literature must often do. I will argue that it is important to read translations in critical awareness of the translator's choices and biases, even if we have no direct knowledge of a text's original language, and such a critically attuned reading can help us to make the most of the reading experience, at times even discovering ways in which a work has gained in translation.

If the opening chapters focus on ways we can reach into the world of the foreign text, the fifth and sixth chapters discuss ways in which authors themselves can reach out beyond their own culture. The fifth chapter looks at works that are set abroad, while the sixth chapter discusses new modes of writing in today's globalizing world. Finally, the epilogue outlines ways in which interested readers can go farther in reading and studying world literature, from primary texts to critical readings to language study and time spent abroad.

This book can be read on its own or as an adjunct to a survey course. The focus on different genres in the opening chapters can dovetail with a genre-based course plan, though the issues raised in each chapter can equally be applied to works in any genre. There is also a movement over the course of the book from early periods to modern times, reflecting the progression typical of many courses, but I often counterpoint early and later materials; a chronological presentation is only one way to set up a course or a plan of reading. In the interest of keeping this book to a manageable length, I have discussed most works fairly briefly, and usually with only tacit relation to the large bodies of scholarship that have grown up around many of them. The discussions here are by no means intended as full-scale readings, but are given as examples of general issues and as portals into extended reading of these and comparable works.

This book aims to illustrate something of the extraordinary variety of world literature, and so it includes discussion of a wide range of writers, including Homer and Sophocles in ancient Greece, Kalidasa in medieval India, Murasaki Shikibu in Heian Japan, and onward to the Turkish novelist Orhan Pamuk, winner of the Nobel Prize in Literature in 2006. Yet I have tried to resist the temptation to pile example upon example; in each chapter, three or four key works form the centerpiece of discussion, with briefer treatments of several more. The examples given here are intended to highlight the problems raised and to suggest major strategies that have been employed by writers and that can be adopted by readers today.

This book treats many texts that have become standard in world literature courses, from *The Epic of Gilgamesh* to Voltaire's *Candide* to Walcott's *Omeros*. Yet I take up less familiar works as well, both to find good examples for a given point and also to showcase writers whom I find particularly fascinating and want more people to read. It can be reassuring to realize that we can get a good first grounding in world literature by attending to the general issues presented by a reasonable number of works. Yet it is also exhilarating to know that a tremendous expanse of possibility opens out before us from that point onward, with field after field offering a far richer and more varied diet than any one literary landscape could possibly provide. James Joyce has a line in *Finnegans Wake* – perhaps the most global text ever written – envisioning an ideal reader with "an ideal insomnia." Perhaps there is no better definition for world literature than the expanding universe of works that compel us to become that ideal reader, dreaming of that ideal insomnia.

Chapter 1

What Is "Literature"?

A first challenge in reading world literature is the fact that the very idea of literature has meant many different things over the centuries and around the world. Even in the English-speaking world today, the term can be applied very broadly or quite restrictively. At its most general, "literature" simply means "written with letters" – really, any text at all. In the examination room following a skiing accident, when your surgeon says "I've pulled up the latest literature on compound fractures," she means medical reports and statistics, not Thomas Mann's novels. In its cultural sense, "literature" refers first and foremost to poems, plays, and prose fiction – works of creative imagination written in heightened and pleasurable language. Yet even in this focused sense, literature's boundaries are blurry. Often readers only admit some poems and novels into the category of "real" literature, including Virginia Woolf but considering Harlequin romances and Stephen King thrillers as subliterary trash. Advertising jingles are rarely assigned in literature courses, even though they represent a minimal form of poetry.

Serious or artistic literature can be described by the term belles-lettres, a phrase suggesting that beauty of language matters more than a literary text's use-value or its direct statements. By contrast, a jingle is not meant to be savored for its beauty; its meter and rhyme are used purely instrumentally, helping the message lodge in your mind so that you'll remember to buy a particular brand of toothpaste. Even in the sense of belles-lettres, though, literature can be defined with varying degrees of breadth. A great essayist like Michel de Montaigne, and eloquent scientific writers such as Charles Darwin or Sigmund Freud, offer many rewards to a reader who gives close attention to their language and to the shaping of ideas and narrative in their works. Freud actually won a leading German literary award, the Goethe Prize, in recognition of the art of his essays and case studies, and he is often taught in literature courses alongside Proust, Kafka, and Woolf.

The boundaries of literature were quite broad in the eighteenth and nineteenth centuries, and though they contracted in the first half of the twentieth, they have steadily widened out again over the past several decades. Literature anthologies now regularly include religious and philosophical texts, essays, autobiographical writing, and examples of creative nonfiction along with poems, plays, and prose fiction. Literature has expanded even beyond its root sense of "written with letters" to include oral compositions by illiterate poets. Movies are often found on literature course syllabi today, even though the dialogue is only one part of the artwork, and often not the most important part. All the same, today's movies give many of the pleasures that novels gave nineteenth-century readers, and "literature" can appropriately be considered in its broad sense to include such works of cinematic narrative.

Many cultures have made no firm distinctions between imaginative literature and other forms of writing. "Belles-lettres" would be a good translation of the ancient Egyptian term *medet nefret*, "beautiful words," but *medet nefret* could refer to any form of rhetorically heightened composition, whether poetry, stories, philosophical dialogues, or political speeches. The classical Chinese term *wen* is translated as "literature" when it refers to poetry and artistic prose, but it carries a much wider set of meanings, including pattern, order, and harmonious design. In view of this variety, we need to prepare ourselves to read different works with different expectations. Primo Levi's haunting *Survival in Auschwitz* would lose much of its force if it ever turned out that Auschwitz had never existed, or that Levi had not been interned there, whereas for readers of Boccaccio's *Decameron* it hardly matters whether there was an actual plague in Florence that forced people to flee the city and start telling each other ribald stories in the countryside.

Within a given literary tradition, authors and readers build up a common fund of expectations as to how to read different kinds of composition, and experienced readers can approach a work with a shared sense of how to take it. Reviewers may praise a popular history of the French Revolution for being "as gripping as a novel," but we will still expect all the events in the book to be documented in sources that the historian has read and not made up. Conversely, the Argentine writer Jorge Luis Borges was famous for devising *ficciones* that often look like sober scholarly reports, but readers soon discover that unlikely or even impossible events are taking place, while many of Borges's "sources" are entirely invented and are part of the fiction themselves. At a middle ground, when we read something subtitled "a historical novel," we assume that it will adhere to the general outlines of a real sequence of events, but we allow the author to take major creative liberties in supplementing historical figures and events with invented characters and scenes.

Writers sometimes deliberately push the envelope with genre-bending experiments, and confusions can arise when we mistake a work's genre or an author's intention, as when Orson Welles broadcast his dramatization of *The War of the Worlds* and some listeners panicked at what they thought was a genuine news report of an alien invasion. Usually, though, a work fits well enough within a form whose rules we know. A lover of Petrarch and Shakespeare can approach Wordsworth's sonnets with a good sense of what a sonnet is (fourteen pentameter lines, typically composed in one of two dominant rhyme schemes, the "Petrarchan" and the "Shakespearean"). With this background, readers can then appreciate Wordsworth's creative use of this classic form and his distinctive departures from it, as when he varies the rhyme scheme for dramatic effect. With world literature, however, we often encounter works that reflect very different literary norms and expectations than our home tradition employs. A close familiarity with Shakespeare's sonnets won't help us much in appreciating the distinctive drama of a *ghazal* – a lyric form popular over many centuries in Persia and north India, with its own set of rules for rhyme and its own assumptions about the ways in which poets experience love and longing and pour out their sorrows in highly ironic verse.

The World of the Text

Quite beyond the varied norms associated with individual literary genres, different cultures have often had distinctive patterns of belief concerning the nature of literature and its role in society. A good deal – though by no means all – of Western literature during the past several hundred years has been markedly individualistic in its emphases. Many modern novels focus on the inner development of a hero or heroine, often in opposition to society as a whole, with the protagonist escaping from social restrictions – like Joyce's Stephen Dedalus – or tragically hemmed in by them – like Flaubert's Madame Bovary. Much of Western literature, as Harold Bloom has put it in *The Western Canon,* is "the image of the individual thinking" (34).

Western lyrics have long taken the form of an individual thinking aloud, as with the following lyric by an anonymous sixteenth-century poet:

> Western wind, when wilt thou blow,
>   The small rain down can rain?
> Christ, if my love were in my arms
>   And I in my bed again!
> (Quiller-Couch 20)

Here, we seem to be overhearing the complaint of an unhappy lover, but the speaker isn't addressing anyone, just the wind, and even the wind is absent from the scene. Nor is the scene itself fully present to us. We don't have any way to know whether the speaker is indoors or outside, pacing about the countryside or gazing through the window of an inn; the focus is strongly on his – or her? – interior state of mind.

Similar emphases can be seen in an otherwise very different poem, "Nombrarte" (Naming you), written four centuries later by the Chilean poet Alejandra Pizarnik:

> No el poema de tu ausencia,
> sólo un dibujo, una grieta en un muro,
> algo en el viento, un sabor amargo.
> (Pizarnik 98)

> [Not the poem of your absence,
> just a sketch, a crack in a wall,
> something in the wind, a bitter aftertaste.]

In many ways, Pizarnik's 1965 poem is radically different from "Western Wind." It has no rhymes and no set meter or number of syllables in a line; it lacks any completed sentences, with no verbs and only a few broken phrases. A sixteenth-century poet would probably not have recognized this as verse at all. The poem even begins by denying that it is "the poem of your absence" that an earlier poet might have composed; it offers no movement, no expected resolution. Instead of a fertile spring wind that can reunite the lovers, here we have an ill wind that blows no one any good and only brings a bitter aftertaste.

Despite these differences, "Nombrarte" resembles "Western Wind" in important respects. Like the sixteenth-century poet, Pizarnik gives us a speaker who is obsessed with an evidently absent lover, and we seem to be inside the speaker's head. The absent lover seems as far away as the western wind was for the earlier speaker. As in the earlier poem, the speaker may be indoors or outside. She – or he? – may only be thinking about walls and winds, or may be feeling a chill breeze while looking at a cracked wall that brings her situation home to her: there is no telling, as the focus once again is on the speaker's interior drama.

A far more social world opens up when we turn to the love poetry written in early India, as can be seen in the following short lyric dating from around the year 800:

> Who wouldn't be angry to see
> his dear wife with her lower lip bitten?
> You scorned my warning to smell
> the bee-holding lotus. Now you must suffer.
>
> (Ingalls 102)

On first reading, this poem seems only a step removed from "Western Wind" and "Nombrarte." Once again, we are overhearing a single speaker, though now talking with someone else, apparently a close friend who has hurt her lip and is afraid that her husband will be upset by her spoiled looks. Though the scene has widened to include the wife, she is silent, and once again we have only the most minimal indications of where the scene is supposed to be set. The conversation may take place in a garden graced with blossoming lotus plants, but it could just as well be occurring indoors, hours later, as the speaker tends her friend's swollen lip.

If we read this poem as we would read the Western examples, we would see it as concerned with the wife's emotional state, taking our cue from the poem's conclusion, which emphasizes her suffering. Yet seen in these Western terms, the poem looks rather slender and unsatisfying, and the sudden introduction of the idea of suffering seems uncalled-for. A bee-sting should really only be a temporary annoyance, and it ought to inspire sympathy rather than anger in any reasonable spouse. Are we to imagine that the wife is married to an abusive husband? Instead of bringing her some lip balm, has he flown off the handle just because the swelling keeps her from kissing him? From Euripides to Joyce Carol Oates, there is a long tradition in the West of literature concerning abusive spouses, so this explanation may come to a Western reader's mind, and yet it hardly seems relevant here. Far from condemning the husband, the friend begins by asserting that anyone would naturally be angry on observing his wife's swollen lip.

The riddle is soon solved if we read farther in Sanskrit poetry, for many Sanskrit *kavyas* or lyric poems concern illicit or adulterous passion. What is more, Indian poets often speak of tell-tale marks from bites or scratches made by lovers in the heat of passion. From the poem's opening couplet, then, a reader of *kavya* poetry would immediately be alerted to the underlying situation: the wife's lover has carelessly bit her in a place she can't conceal. The husband's anger, and the wife's suffering, follow naturally from this revealing mistake, and the poet's skill is seen in his playful use of a classic motif.

This much can be learned about the poem's context by reading a collection of Sanskrit love poetry, but it is also possible to avail ourselves of more explicit commentary, for in the Sanskrit tradition scholar-poets wrote elaborate treatises on poetic language. This poem was discussed in around the year 1000 by one of the greatest Sanskrit commentators, a scholar named Abhinavagupta. What his interpretation shows is how intensely social this poetry was seen to be. Abhinavagupta never considers that the poem features a pair of friends and no one else. Instead, what at first looks like a private conversation turns out to be overflowing with social drama:

> The meaning of the stanza is as follows. An unfaithful wife has had her lip bitten by a lover. To save her from her husband's reproaches she is here addressed by a clever female friend, who knows that the husband is nearby but pretends not to see him. *Now you must suffer*: the literal sense is directed to the adulterous wife. The suggested sense, on the other hand, is directed to the husband and informs him that she is not guilty of the offense. (Ingalls 103)

Abhinavagupta's reading immediately opens out the poem beyond the individual or two-person focus we might expect from a Western lyric. At this point we may still find comparisons to European fiction and drama, in the kind of double dealing found in Boccaccio and Molière, whose adulterous heroines and sly servants often direct two levels of meaning at differing recipients. But Abhinavagupta is only just beginning to describe the scene as he understands it. "There is also a suggestion," he continues, "directed to the neighbors who, if they hear the wife being roundly abused by the husband, may suspect her of misconduct." And more than that: "There is a suggestion directed to her fellow wife, who would be delighted by the abuse of her rival and by [the news of] her adultery. The suggestion lies in the word *dear* ('dear wife'), which shows that the wife addressed is the more attractive."

The garden is getting a little crowded by now, but there is more to come. "There is a suggestion to the adulterous friend of the speaker, informing her, 'You should not take on humiliation at the thought of being accused of bad character in front of your fellow wife; rather, you should take to yourself high esteem and now shine forth.'" And next, "To the wife's secret lover there is a suggestion, telling him that 'Today I have thus saved your heart's beloved who loves you in secret, but you must not bite her again in a place that is so obvious.'" And last of all, "To anyone clever who is standing nearby the speaker's cleverness is suggested, [as though she were to say,] 'This is the way I have concealed things'" (103). Clearly, we are in a different poetic world than the one in which the lonely lover plaineth in the spring.

Important though they are, the contrasts between the English lyric and the Sanskrit poem are differences of degree rather than reflections of some absolute, unbridgeable gulf between East and West. Some Western poems involve more than one or two characters, and not every *kavya* depends upon a landscape as crowded as Abhinavagupta claims. Even for this poem, the key insight is that the jealous husband is within earshot, as this reveals the poem's fundamental drama. It is far from certain that an entire crowd is ringing the garden, ears aflutter. When Abhinavagupta goes so far as to interpret the word "dear" as indicating that there is a less-beloved second wife at hand, he may be indulging in a perennial scholarly temptation – the drive to find some special meaning in every single word of a poem. This urge already surfaced two thousand years ago in rabbinical interpretations of the Bible, whose every grammatical particle was mined for some deep truth, while in modern times professors at Oxford and Yale excel at unfolding surprising meanings in the slightest turn of phrase in Keats. Perhaps the Sanskrit poet was not referring to polygamy at all, but called the wife "dear" in order to underscore the depth of the jealous husband's concern. Perhaps the poet just needed a word to fill out the line.

Even if we take Abhinavagupta's interpretation with a grain of salt, his reading shows that the social world is far more fully present in the poem than a Western-trained reader might have thought. Realizing this difference enables us to make sense of elements that otherwise would seem inconsistent or pointless, and allows us to appreciate the poem as a fascinating elaboration of its tradition's resources. When reading world literature we should beware of the perils of exoticism and assimilation, the two extremes on the spectrum of difference and similarity. We won't get very far if we take the Sanskrit poem as the product of some mysterious Orient whose artists are naïve and illogical, or whose people feel an entirely different set of emotions than we do. On that assumption, we might experience the poem as charming but pointless, either lacking any real focus or else oddly over-dramatizing a minor annoyance as a cause for suffering. Equally, though, we should be wary of assuming that the medieval Sanskrit poet and his audience were *just like us*, playing by the same rules and with the same sorts of cultural assumptions we might find in a contemporary poem about spousal abuse. We need to learn enough about the tradition to achieve an overall understanding of its patterns of reference and its assumptions about the world, the text, and the reader.

Reading the Sanskrit poem can illustrate one basic means of coming to terms with the difference of a foreign work: to pause at moments that seem illogical, overdone, or oddly flat, and ask what is really going on. Not all such moments will yield dramatic insights, of course, either because the confusion can only be cleared up with some detailed specialized knowledge that we lack, or else because the poet has actually stumbled; even Homer sometimes nods, as Alexander Pope famously remarked. Yet with any new work, and particularly with those from a distant time or place, a good assumption is that moments that seem puzzling or absurd on first reading can be windows into the writer's distinctive methods and assumptions. Pausing over the surprising emphasis on the husband's anger, and looking for comparable moments in other works in the same tradition, can reveal the real trouble with the wife's swollen lip. Then we can see how beautifully the poet has modulated the traditions available in that culture, in order to give a unique expression to concerns that can appropriately be described as universal.

The Author's Role

If different cultures have different understandings of the world that a literary text engages, they also diverge in their conception of the ways in which texts are created to begin with. In the Western tradition going back to Plato and Aristotle, literature is something a poet or writer *makes up* – an

13

assumption built into our very terms "poetry" (from Greek *poiesis*, "making") and "fiction" (from Latin *facere*, "to make"). This conception can involve celebrating the writer's supreme creativity, but it can also place literature on a spectrum shading over toward unreality, falsehood, and outright lying. This is why Plato wanted poetry banished from his Republic, whereas Aristotle celebrated poetry as more philosophical than historical writing, able to convey higher truths free from the accidents of everyday life.

By contrast, various cultures have seen literature as deeply embedded in reality, neither above nor below the audience's own physical and moral world. Writers are regarded not as making things up but as observing and reflecting on what they see around them. Stephen Owen has emphasized this difference in discussing the poetics of the Tang Dynasty (618–907), often considered the greatest period of Chinese poetry. In his book *Traditional Chinese Poetry and Poetics*, Owen quotes a poem by the eighth-century poet Du Fu:

> Slender grasses, breeze faint on the shore,
> Here, the looming mast, the lone night boat.
> Stars hang down on the breadth of the plain,
> The moon gushes in the great river's current.
> My name shall not be known from my writing;
> Sick, growing old, I must yield up my post.
> Wind-tossed, fluttering – what is my likeness?
> In Heaven and Earth, a single gull of the sands.
>   (Owen 12)

Unlike the Sanskrit poem, Du Fu's lyric presents the soliloquy of a solitary observer, and in this respect it resembles many Western poems. Yet the speaker is part of the natural world around him; far from fading away before the poet's interior drama of illness, aging, and political regrets, the landscape is shown in detail, its physical features corresponding to the poet's private concerns and memories. As Owen comments, Du Fu's lines "might be a special kind of diary entry, differing from common diary in their intensity and immediacy, in their presentation of an experience occurring at that very moment" (13). Responding to this immediacy of observation, the poem's readers would have taken the speaker to be Du Fu himself, not an unknown, invented persona. Tang Dynasty poets understood their task as conveying to their readers their personal experiences and reflections, artistically shaped and given permanent value through the resources of the poetic tradition.

Very differently, Western writers have often asserted their artistic independence from the world around them. They have regularly insisted that their works do not make declarative statements, sometimes even claiming that they don't say anything at all: "A poem should not mean / But be," as Archibald MacLeish declared in his "Ars Poetica" in 1926 (MacLeish 847). Three and a half centuries earlier, Sir Philip Sidney expressed a similar view in his *Defense of Poesy*: "Now, for the poet, he nothing affirms, and therefore never lieth" (Sidney 517). By contrast, Du Fu's readers were sure that the poet was affirming the truth of his experience; he had indeed written his poem late in life, in exile, on a night when he observed slender grasses swaying and a single gull on the sand, lit by the light of the moon. In his *Apology*, Sidney speaks of the poet's task as "counterfeiting," whereas Du Fu's contemporaries saw him as perceiving the deep correspondences linking heaven, earth, grasses, seagull, and poet.

Like the Sanskrit tradition, Chinese poetry presents a difference in degree rather than a difference in kind from the Western tradition. Du Fu's readers knew that poets never simply transcribed whatever caught their eye; classical Chinese poems are elaborate constructions, in which the poet very selectively weaves elements from the world around him into poetic forms that employ long-cherished images, metaphors, and historical references. Equally, despite all the emphasis on counterfeiting and artifice, Western writers have rarely gone as far as Archibald MacLeish in asserting that their works have no cognitive meaning – a paradoxical stance even for MacLeish, after all, since his poem is making a meaningful statement when it asserts that poems should not mean but be.

There have always been poets in the Western tradition who seem to be recounting their own experiences as Du Fu does. As early as the seventh century BCE, the great Greek poet Sappho certainly wrote as though she was describing just what she felt when she saw a woman she loved flirting with a handsome young man:

> To me it seems
> that man has the fortune of gods,
> whoever sits beside you, and close,
> who listens to you sweetly speaking
> and laughing temptingly;
> my heart flutters in my breast,
> whenever I look quickly, for a moment –
> I say nothing, my tongue broken,
> a delicate fire runs under my skin,

> my eyes see nothing, my ears roar,
> cold sweat rushes down me,
> trembling seizes me,
> I am greener than grass,
> to myself I seem
> needing but little to die.
>
> (Caws 304–5)

Even here, though, Sappho is mixing literal observations with artifice-laden metaphors. She may be green with envy, but surely she has not turned greener than the grass. She has lost her voice, but her tongue isn't physically "broken"; she feels flushed and hears a ringing in her ears, but she isn't actually bursting into flames.

Modes of Reading

The contrasts between Du Fu and Sappho partly reflect differences in the way poets pursued their vocation in their respective cultures, but they are also differences in modes of reading and reception. In comparing Chinese and Western poetic assumptions, Stephen Owen contrasts Du Fu's evening scene with William Wordsworth's sonnet "Composed upon Westminster Bridge, September 3, 1802." Like Du Fu, Wordsworth contemplates an outdoor scene:

> Earth has not anything to show more fair:
> Dull would he be of soul who could pass by
> A sight so touching in its majesty:
> This City now doth, like a garment, wear
> The beauty of the morning; silent, bare,
> Ships, towers, domes, theatres, and temples lie
> Open unto the fields, and to the sky;
> All bright and glittering in the smokeless air.
>
> (Wordsworth 1:460)

Despite the specificity of the poem's title, though, Owen proposes that "it does not matter whether Wordsworth saw the scene, vaguely remembered it, or constructed it from his imagination. The words of the poem are not directed to a historical London in its infinite particularity; the words lead you to something else, to some significance in which the number of vessels on the Thames is utterly irrelevant. That significance is elusive, its fullness eternally out of reach." Whether the poem concerns the force of solitary vision, or nature versus an industrial society, or some other theme, Owen says, "the text points to a plenitude of potential significance, but it does not point to London, at dawn, September 3, 1802" (Owen 13–14).

But why couldn't the poem be read as pointing to London on September 3, 1802? It is true that Wordsworth isn't inviting us to count the number of masts on the Thames, but neither was Du Fu counting blades of grass. The closing lines of Wordsworth's sonnet insistently proclaim the uniqueness of the moment that he is recording:

> Never did sun more beautifully steep
> In his first splendour, valley, rock, or hill;
> Ne'er saw I, never felt, a calm so deep!
> The river glideth at his own sweet will:
> Dear God! the very houses seem asleep;
> And all that mighty heart is lying still!
> (Wordsworth 1:460)

In these lines, Wordsworth invites his reader to share the scene that lies before his eyes. While he could certainly have recorded his impressions long afterward, or even invented the scene outright, Du Fu too could have dreamed up his evening scene, or written about it the next day. The difference concerns the reader's assumptions as much as the poet's own practice.

These assumptions can shift over time within a culture as well as varying between cultures. During the nineteenth century, readers regularly regarded the Romantic poets' verses as closely reflecting their personal experiences. Keats's "Ode to a Nightingale," written in 1819 when "half in love with easeful Death" (Keats 97), was understood as expressing the melancholy of the consumptive poet as he sensed the approach of his early death. More recent readers have sometimes preferred to emphasize the poem's artifice – the ode closes with the speaker unsure whether he has really heard a nightingale or instead has had "a vision or a waking dream" – but Keats's contemporaries did not doubt that he was moved to reflect on beauty and mortality by the sound of a real nightingale pouring forth its soul in ecstasy in the fading light of dusk.

Chinese poets often composed their verses for social occasions, but "occasional verses" have long been written in the West as well. Byron recorded many of his experiences in verses with titles such as "On This Day I Complete My Thirty-Sixth Year: Missolonghi, Jan. 22, 1824" – a poem whose impact depends on the reader's awareness that Byron really was writing from the Greek town named in his subtitle, where he had gone to fight in the cause of Greek independence. Even when Byron wrote about medieval knights or Spanish seducers, his "Byronic heroes" were thinly disguised versions of their creator. Childe Harold's musings and Don Juan's sexual escapades were seen as virtual entries from Byron's journal, a viewpoint encouraged by many ironic asides within the poems.

For much of the twentieth century, on the other hand, literary critics often preferred to regard literary works as what William Wimsatt labeled "verbal icons": self-contained artifacts whose meaning ought to be wholly expressed within the work itself, independent of biographical knowledge. Since the 1980s, however, literary studies have increasingly striven to return literary works to their original social, political, and biographical contexts, and in such readings it can once again make a difference whether Wordsworth's sonnet was or was not truly written on September 3, 1802.

As a matter of fact, it probably wasn't. William's sister Dorothy accompanied him on the trip during which he was struck by the sight of early-morning London from Westminster Bridge. She recorded the event in her diary for July 31, 1802, five weeks before the date given in Wordsworth's title:

> After various troubles and disasters, we left London on Saturday morning at $^1/_2$-past 5 or 6. . . . We mounted the Dover Coach at Charing Cross. It was a beautiful morning. The City, St Pauls, with the River and a multitude of little Boats, made a most beautiful sight as we crossed Westminster Bridge. . . . there was even something like the purity of one of nature's own grand spectacles. (Darbishire 194)

The shifting of the date suggests that the sonnet is not after all an "occasional poem" composed when Wordsworth had the perception he describes; even if the poem was first drafted in July, Wordsworth later brought its date forward in a significant way. For in late July, he was taking the Dover Coach on his way to spend a month in France, where he had lived for a year in 1791–2 during the heady early days of the French Revolution and had shared the revolutionaries' hopes for a radical remaking of society – hopes later dashed in the Reign of Terror and its imperial Napoleonic aftermath.

During his stay in revolutionary France, Wordsworth had plunged into an intense love affair with a Frenchwoman, Annette Vallon; their liaison had produced a daughter, Caroline, before Wordsworth's family had insisted he return home. In July 1802, engaged to be married in England, he was making a trip back to France to settle affairs with Annette; he would be seeing his daughter for the first time since her infancy a decade before. During this trip he wrote a series of sonnets filled with regret about the course of the Revolution and – less obviously – about his failed romance with Annette Vallon and his brief reacquaintance with their daughter. Caroline appears, for instance, as the unidentified child in his sonnet "It Is a Beauteous Evening, Calm and Free," set on the beach at Calais:

> Dear Child! dear Girl! that walkest with me here,
> If thou appear untouched by solemn thought,
> Thy nature is not therefore less divine:
> Thou liest in Abraham's bosom all the year;
> And worshipp'st at the Temple's inner shrine,
> God being with thee when we know it not.
> (Wordsworth 1:444)

Read biographically, this poem expresses Wordsworth's ambivalent relief that Caroline is doing well without him, and if he can only visit very infrequently, she can have the patriarch Abraham holding her all year round.

The visit with Annette before his impending marriage cannot have been easy, and Wordsworth was ready to get away after a decent interval. In a sonnet "Composed by the Sea-side, near Calais, August, 1802," Wordsworth thinks longingly of returning home: "I, with many a fear / For my dear Country, many heartfelt sighs, / Among men who do not love her, linger here" (Wordsworth 2:40). A companion piece, "Composed in the Valley near Dover, on the Day of Landing," expresses his feelings on his return to England: "Here, on our native soil, we breathe once more," the sonnet begins. In place of the daughter left behind in France, Wordsworth comforts himself with the sight of English boys at play: "those boys who in yon meadow-ground / In white-sleeved shirts are playing; and the roar / Of the waves breaking on the chalky shore; — / All, all are English." Home from the brief reunion with the lover of his youth, Wordsworth now experiences "one hour's perfect bliss" with a different woman – his sister, Dorothy:

> Thou are free,
> My Country! and 'tis joy enough and pride
> For one hour's perfect bliss, to tread the grass
> Of England once again, and hear and see,
> With such a dear Companion at my side. (2:43–4)

Wordsworth, then, can be read like Du Fu as conveying his personal experiences and observations, rather than as representing the imaginary thoughts of an invented persona. Admittedly, Wordsworth refers only very obliquely to his romantic entanglements; though he specifies dates and places, the sonnets never mention Annette, Caroline, or even his sister by name. Instead, Wordsworth develops his private drama into a contrast of English peace and freedom versus French turmoil and tyranny. Yet Du Fu also was typically indirect in alluding to his major source of unhappiness, the failure of his political ambitions and his banishment from the imperial court: he never names the Emperor or his political rivals, any more than Wordsworth is prepared to name Annette and Caroline.

The fundamental difference between the poet's role in the Chinese and English traditions, then, involves ways of reading as much as poetic practice. Yet the resulting poems do read quite differently, making different demands and assuming different habits of reading on our part. Du Fu's poems are inseparable from his life, whereas to read Wordsworth's sonnets against his biography is to make a choice that the poems sometimes hint at but never openly invite. In referring to a "dear Child" and a "dear Companion" in place of Caroline and Dorothy, Wordsworth may be offering an obscure half-confession, but he can also be giving his readers a purposefully limited view into his life. The sonnets' themes require him to have a child and then a contrasting adult companion at his side, but the reader is not meant to be distracted by an overabundance of personal detail, which Wordsworth would have regarded as egotistical self-display.

By leaving the identities open, Wordsworth hopes to make his sonnets resonate more strongly for his readers, who can insert the faces of their own beloved children and companions in place of his. The shifting of the date of the Westminster Bridge sonnet, then, was something other than an act of autobiographical bad faith. Wordsworth's redating of the poem enabled him to place it at a time appropriate to the sonnet's poetic mood, the period of relieved return rather than the anxious point of departure. Altering the facts of his life even as he builds on them, Wordsworth is still working within the Western tradition of the poet as the maker of fictions.

Among the most famous of Du Fu's poems is a sequence of lyrics known under the overall title of "Autumn Meditations." These poems contain lines that could come from Wordsworth's sonnet cycle: "A thousand houses rimmed by the mountains are quiet in the morning light, / Day after day in the house by the river I sit in the blue of the hills. / . . . My native country, untroubled times, are always in my thoughts" (Graham 53). Closely though Du Fu and Wordsworth may converge in such observations, their methods are sharply different. Wordsworth served his poetic purposes by transposing "Westminster Bridge" from summer to autumn, but such a shift of timing would be nearly inconceivable in the Chinese tradition. It never would have occurred to Du Fu to write an autumn sequence in mid-summer, or to take a summer experience and place it in the autumn. Such a transposition would almost certainly have produced poetic absurdities if he had attempted it, as Chinese poetry is closely attuned to the passing seasons. Flowers, migrating birds, seasonal occupations, and more would have to change. Even with such changes, the very tone of a summer poem would have seemed jarring in an autumn setting, so a summer scene simply could not be passed off as an autumn event.

What Is a Novel?

Different expectations about literature vary the relations among genres in different cultures' literary ecosystems. Western readers, for example, have long been accustomed to think of poetry and prose as clearly distinct modes of writing; the very terms "prosaic" and "poetic" are typically regarded as polar opposites. In the later nineteenth century, various writers began to push against this distinction, writing more self-consciously poetic prose and sometimes composing "prose poems." Yet these experiments have been the exception rather than the norm, and it can take some adjustment to read works from cultures that mix poetry more openly into prose than is usually the case in the West.

One of the greatest of all prose fictions is *The Tale of Genji*, written shortly after the year 1000 by a woman in the Japanese imperial court writing under the pen name "Murasaki Shikibu." She interspersed nearly 800 poems through her book's fifty-four chapters, and Western readers have not always known what to make of the mixed result. Arthur Waley, who first translated *Genji* into English in the 1920s, excised most of the poetry outright, and translated the surviving lyrics as prose. In so doing, Waley made the *Genji* look more like a European novel and helped keep attention focused on the unfolding story. Yet his choice went dramatically against the work's traditional reception, for Murasaki's poems were always regarded in Japan as central to her text. As early as the twelfth century, the great poet Fujiwara no Shunjei asserted that every would-be poet must read the *Genji* (Murasaki xiii). Often people didn't bother with the sprawling narrative as a whole, but read excerpts centered on particularly well-loved poems.

The predominance of poetic values in Japanese literary circles had major consequences for Murasaki's practice as a writer of prose. Not only is her story built around poetic moments, but Murasaki shows relatively little interest in such staples of Western fiction as character development and plot. Her lead characters, Genji and his child-bride Murasaki – from whom Murasaki Shikibu took her own pen name – die two-thirds of the way through the book, which then starts up again with a new set of characters in the next generation. The story reaches a kind of tentative stopping-point in its fifty-fourth chapter, but it does not end in any way that readers of Western novels would expect. Even if Murasaki might have intended to carry the story further, it does not appear that a climactic "novelistic" ending was ever an integral part of her plan.

Murasaki also presents her characters more poetically than novelistically. The characters are usually not even identified by name but by shifting series of epithets, often derived from lines in poems they quote or write. Not a proper name at all, for instance, *murasaki* means "lavender," a key word in several poems associated with Genji's love affairs. Indeed, "Murasaki" actually first appears as the epithet for Genji's first love, Fujitsubo, and only later is transferred to the tale's principal heroine. Most translators from Waley onward have settled on fixed names for the characters, but in the original it is only minor, lower-ranking figures who have set names. "The shining Genji" is mostly referred to by a series of different epithets, and the very name "Genji" merely means "bearer of the name" (of Minamoto), a surname bestowed on him – as an illegitimate child – by his emperor father. Genji, in short, is *a* genji, a son who is recognized but excluded from the imperial family. As vividly as Murasaki develops her major characters, they continue to suggest general qualities as they play out recurrent patterns that emerge in generation after generation, in a narrative unfolding of poetic moments of fellowship, longing, rivalry, and reverie.

*

Reading Wordsworth, Du Fu, Sappho, and Murasaki Shikibu together, we can explore the distinctive ways in which these writers transmuted social and emotional turmoil into reflective works of art. Different traditions locate writers differently along the sliding scale between independence from society and integration within it, and a given tradition's writers will be found at various places on their culture's bandwidth on the spectrum, distinctively expressing fundamentally common concerns – political upheaval, romantic loss – that they link to elements from their lived environment: rivers, boats, birds, sunlight, and moonlight.

Even on a first reading, we can appreciate many of these commonalities and be intrigued by the differences we perceive. The challenge as we read and reread is to enter more deeply into the specificity of what each poet is doing. We can do so by attending to formal statements on literary art when a culture has produced critics and poeticians like Aristotle or Abhinavagupta, but even when such explicit statements are lacking, we can read around within a tradition to gain a sense of its coordinates – its writers' characteristic forms, metaphors, and methods. It is much better to begin by reading two or three dozen Tang Dynasty poems than just one or two, seeing Du Fu more clearly, for example, by comparison and contrast to his great contemporaries Li Bo, Wang Wei, and Han Yu. It is not necessary, though, to read hundreds and hundreds of poems in order to get our bearings and develop an intelligent first appreciation of a tradition. Our understanding can always be refined and deepened through further reading, but the essential first step is to gain enough of a foothold in a tradition that an initially flat picture opens out into three dimensions. When this happens, we can pass through the looking-glass and enter into a new literary world – the first and greatest pleasure of the encounter with world literature.

Chapter 2

Reading across Time

The foundational classics of literature come to us from the past. Even within a single national tradition, we need to develop skills in reading across time: students of English literature encounter distant worldviews in *Beowulf* and thickets of strange-looking words in *The Canterbury Tales*. Indeed, the English language itself didn't yet exist when an Anglo-Saxon poet composed *Beowulf* more than a thousand years ago, and we no longer speak the Middle English of Chaucer's pilgrims. "The past is a foreign country," L. P. Hartley wrote in his novel *The Go-Between*; "they do things differently there" (3).

This archaic foreignness becomes all the greater when we look to the world's oldest literary cultures. The history of literature extends back to the earliest Sumerian poetry and the Pyramid Texts of ancient Egypt; within Europe, literature began to take shape with the Homeric epics, written down some 2,800 years ago. Homer is fundamentally foreign even in his own country today, a point made in "Upon a Foreign Verse," by the Greek poet George Seferis:

> And again and again the shade of Odysseus appears before me, his eyes
> red from the waves' salt,
> from his ripe longing to see once more the smoke ascending from
> his warm hearth and the dog grown old waiting by the door.
> A large man, whispering through his whitened beard words in
> our language spoken as it was three thousand years ago.
>
> (Seferis 46–7)

For Seferis, Odysseus is an image of his culture's memory: "He tells me of the harsh pain you feel when the ship's sails swell with memory and your soul becomes a rudder; / . . . and of how strangely you gain strength conversing with the dead when the living who remain are no longer enough" (48). So ancient as to seem a foreigner to his twentieth-century successor, Odysseus also speaks "humbly and calmly," Seferis says, "as though he were my father." The epic's great hero is both near and far in time. The poem ends with Odysseus presenting the poet a timeless gift, a vision of the sea: "He speaks . . . I still see his hands that knew how to judge the carving of the mermaid at the prow / presenting me the waveless blue sea in the heart of winter" (48).

Like many great ancient works, *The Odyssey* is both profoundly foreign and also strangely familiar. In reading across time, we need to keep both aspects alive, neither submerging ourselves in antiquarian details nor absorbing the work so fully into our own world that we mistake *The Odyssey* for a modern novel or look to it for the same pleasures we expect from movies and television today. Not that the Homeric epics are entirely unrelated to novels and mini-series: the eighteenth- and nineteenth-century writers who developed the modern novel were mostly steeped in classical education, and their ideas of how to tell an extended story were significantly shaped by Homer, Virgil, and their epic successors. Much television writing in turn adapts themes and techniques of nineteenth-century realism to the possibilities of the new medium.

One of the fascinations of reading across time is the opportunity to trace the unfolding of situations, characters, themes, and images across the centuries, in the work of writers who knew and responded to their predecessors. This chapter will explore the kinds of continuity and change we can encounter over time, as stories and metaphors evolve across centuries and languages within a varied but broadly connected tradition. We will begin by tracing the development of the Western epic tradition from its earliest manifestations onward, looking at the interplay of oral tradition and literacy and at changing representations of the gods and the underworld. The chapter will close by reversing direction, tracing a poetic motif from the present back into the deep past. Life moves always forward, but literary time is reversible, and as readers of world literature we should become adept at time travel in both directions.

From Orature to Literature

In the broad sweep of human social life, writing is a fairly recent invention: people must have been singing songs and telling tales for many thousands of years before anyone ever devised a means to record their words. We are used today to thinking of literature as something an author *writes*, but the earliest written works were usually versions of songs or stories that had been orally composed and transmitted. Oral compositions often work differently than purely literary works. Even after poets began to compose with stylus or pen in hand, they often adapted old oral techniques to new uses, and important elements of their work can best be understood as holdovers or creative transformations of oral techniques. Epic poems show particularly elaborate uses of oral devices, many of which were developed to aid poets in rapidly composing lines of an ongoing story, and to help illiterate performers remember a long narrative.

Oral composition, often called "orature," has continued in modern times in many regions of the world. In Seferis's poem "Upon a Foreign Verse," Odysseus reminds the speaker of "certain old sailors of my childhood who, leaning on their nets with winter coming on and the wind angering, / used to recite, with tears in their eyes, the song of Erotokritos" – an epic about a valiant knight and his love for the princess Aretousa, composed in Crete in the seventeenth century (Seferis 47). In West Africa, performers continue to recite the epic story of Son-Jara or Sundiata, legendary founder of the Mali empire in around 1250. Though this epic material has been retold and reworked for centuries, contemporary versions can reflect very recent developments. In a performance recorded in 1968, the bard Fa-Digi Sisòkò incorporates into his verse an invitation from a local folklorist, as his assistant vouches for the truth of his words:

> God is the King!
> A man of power . . .   (That's the truth)
> Mansa Magan came for me,   (Indeed)
> A letter was given to me,
> Saying I should speak on Radio Mali,   (Indeed, that happened!
> To sing the praises of Fa-Koli.   That really happened!)
>   (Johnson 84)

The oldest mode of poetic composition takes on new life in the modern medium of radio.

First composed centuries before the alphabet came to Greece, the Homeric epics depict poetry as purely oral in nature, performed in public by professional bards or rhapsodes at banquets. An extended scene of oral performance involves a blind bard named Demodocus ("Leader of the People"), who entertains the royal court on the island of Phaeacia, where

[handwritten margin note: Such as all the repetition in the various versions of Gilgamesh]

26

Odysseus has been shipwrecked as he tries to sail home from Troy. Having prompted Demodocus to sing an episode of the Trojan War, Odysseus praises Demodocus's art, in a warm portrayal of the scene of performance:

> what a fine thing it is to listen to such a bard
> as we have here – the man sings like a god.
> The crown of life, I'd say. There's nothing better
> than when deep joy holds sway throughout the realm
> and banqueters up and down the palace sit in ranks,
> enthralled to hear the bard, and before them all, the tables
> heaped with bread and meats, and drawing wine from a mixing-bowl
> the steward makes his rounds and keeps the winecups flowing.
> This, to my mind, is the best that life can offer.
>
> (*Odyssey* 9:3–11, tr. Fagles)

Odysseus goes on to restore his own life's fortunes by an artful retelling of his perilous adventures since leaving Troy. Filled with sympathy, the king of Phaeacia gives him the best he can offer in return: free transport home, in a ship filled with treasure.

Interestingly, the Homeric poet feels no need to mark any difference between Demodocus's song and Odysseus's tale of his adventures: both appear in the same stately hexameters, even though it appears that Odysseus is simply speaking in prose, rather than singing in elevated verse. Odysseus is a crafty and persuasive talker, but he is no poet strumming a ringing lyre, nor is he performing like Demodocus "flanked by boys in the flush of youth, skilled dancers / who stamped the ground with marvelous pulsing steps" (8:97–8). The difference between Odysseus and Demodocus, however, could readily have been marked in performance. Even if he didn't cue in a floor show when he got to Demodocus's scene, the rhapsode could have used a sweeter voice and a different melody to convey Demodocus's heightened lyricism in contrast to the "ordinary" speech of the other characters. As a result, the poet didn't need to break the stride of his verse; though the difference between Demodocus and Odysseus is flattened out on the page, it would have been fleshed out in a good oral performance.

It was long assumed that Homer (or the poet or poets traditionally known under that name) must have composed *The Iliad* and *The Odyssey* in writing, as each epic is on the order of 12,000 lines long, and it was thought that no one could ever memorize so much. But in the early twentieth century, the classicist Milman Parry found that illiterate bards in Yugoslavia were composing and singing epic poems several thousand lines in length, often using oral techniques that can be seen in the Homeric poems as well. Notably, the Yugoslavian bards didn't need to memorize their poems word for word; rather, they freely improvised on a set base of material, filling out the lines as they went along. They used typical scenes that could be adapted to different settings; they employed stock phrases and formulas of different length that could be used according to how many beats were needed to fill out a line; and they built up patterns of repetition, including "ring composition" whereby scenes or parts of scenes could be nested inside one another and better kept track of that way.

Long before the Homeric age, many of the devices analyzed by Parry were being employed in ancient Mesopotamia. The earliest poetry to be written down was composed by the Sumerians, who invented cuneiform writing in around 3200 BCE. Sumerian poetry is strongly oral in character, employing repetitions that can seem excessive at first sight on the page, but which create an incantatory effect when read aloud:

> Last night, as I, the queen, was shining bright,
> Last night, as I, the queen of heaven, was shining bright,
> As I was shining bright, as I was dancing about,
> As I was uttering a song at the brightening of the oncoming night,
> He met me, he met me,
> The Lord Kuli-Anna met me,
> The lord put his hand into my hand,
> Ushumgalanna embraced me.
>
> (Pritchard 639–40)

As in Homer, epithets vary according to the needs of the meter: at different points in the poem the queen's consort is called Kuli-Anna, Ushumgalanna, or Amaushumgalanna, depending on whether the poet needs four, five, or six syllables to fill out the line.

The Sumerians were gradually absorbed into the states created in southern Mesopotamia by speakers of a different language, Akkadian. When they came to write literary works of their own, often reworking older Sumerian poems, these later poets were immersed in a culture of writing, and they wrote works that were as likely to be read and studied in textual form as to be recited and heard aloud. The greatest epic poem of ancient Mesopotamia, *The Epic of Gilgamesh*, evolved in several stages, from an early cycle of songs in Sumerian to an Akkadian epic written in around 1800 BCE, to a final, expansive version written in around 1200, attributed to a scribe named

Sin-leqe-unninni. This late version of the epic is explicitly literary: it includes a prologue that declares that the poem's hero himself "set all his labours on a tablet of stone." The epic's audience is invited to read the story from a written text:

> See the tablet-box of cedar,
>   release its clasp of bronze!
> Lift the lid of its secret,
>   pick up the tablet of lapis lazuli and read out
> the travails of Gilgamesh, all that he went through.
>
> (George 1–2)

In this highly literate poem, old oral devices of repetition and set scenes are used to newly literary effect. As he ventures into the wilderness to confront the demon guardian of a cedar forest, for example, Gilgamesh has a series of three dreams, each more ominous than the last. Not only does this repetition provide mounting suspense, but the sequence of dreams gives the poet an opportunity to develop the relationship of Gilgamesh to his faithful companion Enkidu, who gives more and more implausible interpretations of the dreams. Though Gilgamesh dreams about being overwhelmed by an avalanche, a raging bull, and a volcano, Enkidu insists that these nightmares anticipate an easy victory over the demon. No longer needed as a memory device, this set of repetitions makes a political and psychological point: as friend and adviser to a headstrong, imperious tyrant, Enkidu cannot resist saying what the king wants to hear, exhibiting progressively worsening judgment as they march into the events that will culminate in Enkidu's own early death.

As the epic tradition developed, it became more fully literary in techniques and quality. Whereas the rhapsodes who performed the Homeric epics were masters of improvisation, the great Roman poet Virgil had the luxury to linger over his lines, pondering the choice and placement of every word, revising his drafts as he pleased. Virgil is famously reported to have asked on his deathbed for his friends to burn the manuscript of *The Aeneid*, since he had wanted to make some final revisions, and he didn't want his masterpiece to go out in unpolished form. Fortunately, Virgil's friends ignored his request, giving the world one of the greatest poems ever written.

Virgil's epic shows many examples of Homeric techniques adapted from oral purposes to new uses. Epithets are musically modulated, stock scenes

29

of battle are varied for thematic effect, and techniques such as ring composition are poetically employed. Whereas Homeric ring composition helped the illiterate poets keep track of large units of narrative, Virgil exploited ring composition to convey sensations of balance, formal order, and fate. Like Odysseus, Aeneas suffers shipwreck and then retells his story to a sympathetic listener, in this case Queen Dido of Carthage, with whom he then has a disastrous love affair before moving on to his destined new homeland of Italy. Like Odysseus as well, Aeneas encounters the story of the Trojan War shortly before he tells his own version. Yet in a sign of the growing literariness of the epic tradition, Virgil doesn't have Aeneas hear his story sung by a bard. Instead, he sees it inscribed on the walls of a temple in the form of a mural. Staring in amazement "at the handiwork / Of artificers and the toil they spent upon it," Aeneas speaks to his companion Achates as tears well up:

> "What spot on earth."
> He said, "what region of earth, Achatës,
> Is not full of the story of our sorrow?
> Look, here is Priam. Even so far away
> Great valor has due honor; they weep here
> For how the world goes, and our life that passes
> Touches their hearts."
>
> (*Aeneid* 1:601–7)

Virgil's mural becomes the next best thing to a literary text, available to be contemplated at leisure. Virgil goes so far as to include a moment of virtual writing on the mural itself, when the young Trojan prince Troilus is mortally wounded in his chariot:

> he clung
> To his warcar, though fallen backward, hanging
> On to the reins still, head dragging on the ground,
> His javelin scribbling S's in the dust. (1:624–7)

This translation's "scribbling S's" nicely picks up the sighing *s* sounds of the Latin original, "versa pulvis inscribitur hasta," literally, "the dust inscribed by the upside-down spear."

Literary values increasingly pervade the later epic tradition. Eventually poetic epic came to be supplanted by extended fictions in prose; the rise of the modern novel was closely linked to print and to the spread of literacy, and no one was expected to recite novels from memory. Yet Victorian families often read novels aloud together, and prose fiction continued to develop in vital interchange with orality. One of the most "written" of all modern novels is James Joyce's *Ulysses*, on whose multiple drafts Joyce worked with a devotion that would have exhausted even Virgil. Written texts fill the pages of Joyce's novel, from the textbooks that the would-be writer Stephen Dedalus uses in the school where he works, to the newspaper advertisements solicited by the novel's Odysseus, Leopold Bloom, to *The Odyssey* itself, whose action structures the novel, unbeknownst to the characters. "*Epi oinopa ponton.* Ah, Dedalus, the Greeks!" Stephen's antagonistic friend Buck Mulligan exclaims. "I must teach you. You must read them in the original" (Joyce 4–5).

Crowded with dozens of physical books and references to hundreds more, Joyce's *Ulysses* is also pervaded by orature of all kinds – from Irish quips and folktales that a visiting Englishman is collecting, to drunken pub conversations with an Odysseus-like sailor, to an aria from Mozart's opera *Don Giovanni*, which Leopold Bloom's wife Molly is practicing for a recital tour she plans to give under the management of her lover Blazes Boylan. Much of the book consists of anecdotes and gossip exchanged among the book's characters. "They are all there, the great talkers," Joyce told the novelist Djuna Barnes in 1922; "they and the things they forgot" (Ellmann 538). Late in life, after decades of self-imposed exile on the Continent, Joyce wrote to a friend that "every day in every way I am walking along the streets of Dublin and along the strand. And 'hearing voices'" (Ellmann 717).

The orality of Homeric tradition figures strongly in the Caribbean poet Derek Walcott's verse novel *Omeros*, whose characters Achille and Hector are illiterate fishermen on Walcott's home island of St. Lucia, rivals for the affections of the beautiful Helen. None of Walcott's St. Lucian characters has ever heard of Homer, but Walcott invokes him as his muse:

> O open this day with the conch's moan, Omeros,
> as you did in my boyhood, when I was a noun
> gently exhaled from the palate of the sunrise. (12)

Walcott's Homer is a figure of orality ("the conch's moan") and also a founding author in the published series of *The World's Great Classics* that Walcott's father used to read in their local barbershop (71). Whereas Virgil introduced the Homeric tradition in the form of a mural of Troy, Walcott takes the art analogy a step further, presenting a bust of Homer himself. This bust is located in the American studio of a Greek artist named Antigone, who tells the poet that "Homer" is called "Omeros" in modern Greek. Appearing as a character in the novel, Walcott repeats the name, translating it into his own oral terms:

> I said, "Omeros,"
>
> and O was the conch-shell's invocation, *mer* was
> both mother and sea in our Antillean patois,
> *os*, a grey bone, and the white surf as it crashes
>
> and spreads its sibilant collar on a lace shore.
> Omeros was the crunch of dry leaves, and the washes
> that echoed from a cave-mouth when the tide has ebbed.
>
> The name stayed in my mouth. (14)

Though Homer signifies a life-giving orality, he is inspiring a self-consciously written text, which often draws attention to its own process of composition. In the scene in which Walcott contemplates the bust of Homer, he is struggling with his artist-lover's impending abandonment of America and of their relationship. When he strokes Antigone's arm, it feels colder than the marble bust, and her words express a longing for Greece, not for him:

> "I'm tired of America, it's time for me to go back
> To Greece, I miss my islands." I write, it returns–
> The way she turned and shook out the black gust of hair. (14)

Writing becomes for Walcott the ultimate medium in which to enshrine Antigone's parting words and "our Antillean patois" alike.

The extraordinary resilience of the Western epic tradition – as of the *Mahabharata* and *Ramayana* in India – testifies to its adaptability in very different circumstances over time. In the following pages, we will look at what might seem to have been the least usable element for later Western poets: the polytheism of the classical world, with its crowded Olympus of powerful, quarreling gods and goddesses, always ready to stir up dramatic conflict on earth. The coming of monotheism already limited the variety of heavenly activities that could be envisioned, though Milton could employ fallen or loyal angels such as Satan and Gabriel in *Paradise Lost* to accomplish many of the tasks that the classical gods and goddesses had once performed, waging war in heaven and intervening on earth. During the Enlightenment and beyond, however, the modern novel developed into a highly secular form. In the early twentieth century, the novel was famously defined by the theorist Georg Lukács as "the epic of a world abandoned by God" (Lukács 20). How did the epic tradition survive the collapse of the heavenly order that had so long framed it?

The Human and the Divine

Lukács's formulation does not actually insist that God is dead, only that he has departed from the earthly scene, and in fact a gradual withdrawal of the gods from the daily lives of mortals can already be seen in the ancient tradition itself, almost as soon as we look beyond Homer. The gods are constantly invoked in Homer and ultimately control the action; during the final battle before the walls of Troy in *The Iliad*, Zeus appears in the sky with a balance, on which he weighs the fates of the adversaries and decrees the Trojan defeat. At the outset of the epic, deprived of honor and an attractive captive by King Agamemnon, Achilles strides along the seashore, praying to his mother, Thetis, for help. She is a sea-nymph, and she hears him from beneath the sea. Moved by maternal pity, she comes to Achilles, sits down beside him, strokes him with her hand, and asks him what is the matter.

The Homeric gods dwell apart from humanity, yet they can instantly bridge this distance and engage in direct physical interaction with mortals – including engendering offspring such as Achilles. Having agreed to help her son, Thetis goes off to appeal to Zeus, enthroned on "the highest peak of rugged Olympus," the meeting-place of heaven and earth. Once there, Thetis grasps Zeus's knees with her left hand so that he can't leave, and takes him by the chin with her right hand, forcing him to look her in the eye as she makes her appeal.

A parallel scene appears in *The Epic of Gilgamesh*, but with significant differences. As Gilgamesh plans a dangerous journey to confront the demon Humbaba at the distant Cedar Forest, he appeals to his mother Ninsun, a minor divinity like Thetis, to intercede on his behalf with the sun god, Shamash. Yet in this epic the hero's mother doesn't physically travel to meet the sun god. Instead, she goes up onto the roof of her house and offers a prayer, acting for all the world like a human priestess:

> She climbed the staircase and went up on the roof,
>   on the roof she set up a censer to Shamash.
> Scattering incense she lifted her arms in appeal to the Sun God:
>   "Why did you afflict my son Gilgamesh with so restless a spirit?
> For now you have touched him and he will tread
>   the distant path to the home of Humbaba.
> He will face a battle he knows not,
>   he will ride a road he knows not."

(George 24)

Ninsun asks Shamash to send his thirteen powerful winds to help Gilgamesh defeat Humbaba. The epic records no direct reply from Shamash – again, reflecting the conditions of human prayer – but the thirteen winds do come to Gilgamesh's aid in the decisive battle, incapacitating the ogre so that Gilgamesh and Enkidu can capture him.

Though *Gilgamesh* and *The Iliad* portray their heavenly encounters differently, they use the goddess's appeal to similar ends. Ninsun's anxiety for her son's safety is paralleled by the fear that Thetis expresses when Achilles asks her to secure Zeus's aid in his struggles:

> Thetis answered him then, letting the tears fall: "Ah me,
> my child. Your birth was bitterness. Why did I raise you?
> If only you could sit by your ships, untroubled, not weeping
> since indeed your lifetime is to be short, of no length.
> Now it has befallen that your life must be brief and bitter
> beyond all men's. To a bad destiny I bore you in my chambers."

(*Iliad* 1:413–18)

In both epics, the fragility of mortal life is dramatized through the concern of the hero's immortal mother. Each hero escapes death for the time being, though his ultimate mortality shadows the entire story. Within the epics, the hero's mortality is transferred to the person of the hero's beloved friend, who does die, tragically, within the frame of the epic's action. In this respect, Enkidu is a direct ancestor of Patroklos, Achilles's intimate friend and lover.

Such parallels are probably not the result of random chance. *The Epic of Gilgamesh* circulated widely throughout the Near East; fragments of its tablets have been found at Megiddo in Palestine and in Asia Minor. There the epic was translated into Hittite, the language of the Trojan Greeks' powerful neighbors in what is now Turkey. As M. L. West has argued in *The East Face of Helicon*, poet-singers were likely performing *Gilgamesh* in

Syria and Cyprus during the period in which the Homeric epics were first being elaborated. Intensive cultural exchanges went on around the ancient Mediterranean world over the centuries, clearly visible in the profound debt that Greek art owes to Persian and Near Eastern traditions. Writing itself reached Greece through Phoenician traders who had adapted early West Semitic alphabets used by Syrian and Canaanite groups. The early Greek bards were illiterate, and no passages in Homer are direct translations of anything in *Gilgamesh*, but it is likely that some bilingual Greek bards heard *Gilgamesh* performed and found themes they could adapt to their own purposes. Through such means of transmission, Achilles and his restless fellow hero Odysseus came to bear a distinct family resemblance to Gilgamesh, their greatest epic predecessor.

An important point can be seen here: a literary tradition may not develop in a linear fashion, unfolding organically like a flower; it may develop by fits and starts, advances and returns. *The Epic of Gilgamesh* reached its final form around 1200 BCE, centuries before *The Iliad* did, but it shows a more distanced, "modern" conception of the interaction of gods and mortals than is found in Homer. As in *Gilgamesh*, people today often light incense and pray to Jesus, or Allah, or the Hindu divinities Shiva and Kali, but we no longer expect that anyone on earth can grasp a god by his knees and force him to look us in the eye. Sin-leqe-unninni, the author of the final form of *Gilgamesh*, is closer to us in some respects than the illiterate Homeric bards centuries after him; he was heir to a thousand years of literary culture, and his audience had come to expect certain standards of earthly realism even when the heavenly gods were involved.

Underworld Dreams

The gods gradually abandoned the earthly stage, but they still wait in the wings in many later works. Even if poets came to doubt their heroes' ability to go up to heaven in person, they have rarely forgotten that everyone will, one day, descend into the earth. A descent into the underworld early on became a central moment in the epic tradition, a way of linking the tale and its hero with the past, and often providing a setting for predictions of the future. Already in antiquity, poets explored the options of giving their heroes a direct entry into a physical underworld or a more indirect means of access, such as in a dream or vision.

In an early Sumerian cycle of poems about Gilgamesh and Enkidu, one poem shows Enkidu descending into the underworld to retrieve a ball that falls into a fissure in the earth; he fails to maintain his disguise as a corpse and is seized by the underworld spirits. The later epic does not reproduce anything like such a literal descent. Instead, when the jealous goddess Ishtar sentences Enkidu to an early death, he has a feverish dream of what awaits him in "the House of Dust," where people eat clay for bread and drink muddy water for beer. This vision suits the expectations of Sin-leqe-unninni's audience that the only way for living people to receive knowledge of the afterlife would be through dream-visions – it no longer seemed plausible for someone to venture into the underworld through a fissure in the ground in order to retrieve a ball. Once Enkidu dies, Gilgamesh then goes in search of the secret of immortality, possessed by his long-lost ancestor Uta-napishtim, sole survivor of the ancient Flood. Gilgamesh's journey includes a march through a dark tunnel, after which he must navigate the Waters of Death, which no mortal before him has ever crossed alive. In his case, the underworld descent is naturalized as a near-death experience.

In the eleventh book of *The Odyssey*, Odysseus has a direct encounter with the dead in what is usually called the *nekuia* or "underworld descent." Yet like Gilgamesh he doesn't exactly descend: he goes to a distant locale and summons up the spirits of the dead, most notably his mother, with whom he has a moving conversation. In the *Aeneid*, on the other hand, Aeneas does physically descend into the classical underworld, where he crosses the river Lethe and then enters the vast city of Dis, god of the underworld. There, he sees the elaborate punishments meted out to such figures as Tantalus, then goes on to meet his dead father, who prophesies his future adventures and outlines the entire history of Rome.

Aeneas's journey takes place within the action of the epic, rather than in a mere dream, and so it reverses the general pattern of a movement away from direct otherworldly adventures. Yet this reversal suggests that, like oral formulas, the underworld descent had become a stock scene by Virgil's time, an element that a full-dress epic ought to have and that the poet could exploit purely for its literary potential. Virgil's reworking of Odysseus's underworld descent is a bravura display of what he can do with the old material; the scene hovers somewhere between a grim reality and a sophisticated literary conceit.

Virgil's readers could fully appreciate his artistry simply by suspending their disbelief, rather than needing to believe that he was giving a reliable roadmap to hell. When Aeneas meets his father in the climactic scene of his underworld descent, he tries to embrace him, only to find his father's image slipping through his fingers, "volucrique simillima somno" – "most like a winged dream" (*Aeneid* 6:702). Significantly, Aeneas's descent concludes with his return to earth through "the gate of dreams," with a melancholy specification that Aeneas returns to earth through "the gate of ivory," which gives false dreams to earth, rather than "the gate of horn," source of true dreams.

Later epic writers continued to exploit the possibilities of visionary descents. Dante's *Divine Comedy* seems at once to be a dream-vision and a literal account of an otherworldly, out-of-body experience. Dante fleshes out his infernal scenes with an intense physicality and a deep psychological realism that refuse to allow us to take refuge in disbelief. Failures of true faith, after all, are what bring souls into hell in the first place. More insistently real than Virgil's underworld, Dante's Inferno nonetheless shows a further distancing of God from the action of the story – not because Dante is voyaging in a world abandoned by God but because the reverse is true: this is the kingdom of those who have chosen to abandon God. God has organized this underworld with elaborate poetic justice, making each torment fit the crime and fulfill the perverted personal inclination of the sinner. In Virgil, Aeneas meets his father Anchises at the climax of his underworld voyage; in Dante, the father-figure becomes Virgil himself, who guides Dante through the Inferno.

In modern times, the heirs of the epic tradition are novelists who won't ordinarily represent their characters as entering the classical or Christian underworld, and yet they continue to showcase epic descents, often in the form of dreams or fantasies. In Joyce's *Ulysses*, Leopold Bloom has recurring visions of his dead son Rudy wandering among the shades of the dead, in a muted version of Virgil's Elysian Fields: "silently the soul is wafted over regions of cycles of generations that have lived. A region where grey twilight ever descends, never falls on wide sagegreen pasturefields, shedding her dusk, scattering a perennial dew of stars" (Joyce 338). Even as Bloom falls into this reverie, the young Stephen Dedalus sits nearby comparing himself to Odysseus: "You have spoken of the past and its phantoms," Stephen says to a friend. "Why think of them? If I call them into life across the waters of Lethe will not the poor ghosts troop to my call? Who supposes it?" (339). Odysseus's summoning of ghosts has here become the would-be novelist's dream of re-creating the Dublin of his youth in a compelling fiction.

If modern characters can still glimpse the classical underworld in dreams, they can also experience the infernal realm closer to home. Many twentieth-century novels use extended patterns of underworld reference to portray a hell on earth. In *Ulysses*, the long "Circe" chapter takes place in Dublin's red-light district, "Night Town," in which infernal visions mingle with snatches of realistic conversation between Stephen, Bloom, and a group of whores in a cheap bordello. A comparable patterning can be found in a 1965 work by the African-American poet Amiri Baraka. His poetic novel *The System of Dante's Hell* overlays Dante's Inferno and the ghetto neighborhoods of Newark, New Jersey. Baraka's book is filled with gritty realism, but his scenes also have a hallucinatory quality, conveyed in swirling, staccato bursts of prose. A chapter called "The Diviners," for example, builds on Dante's choice of symbolic punishment for fortunetellers, who are deformed in hell by having their heads turned to face backward:

> Gypsies lived here before me. Heads twisted backwards, out to the yards, stalks. Their brown garages, stocking caps, green Bird suits. Basil suits. 15 feet to the yard, closer from the smashed toilet. Year of the Hurricane. Year of the Plague. Year of the Dead Animals. . . .
>
> You can never be sure of the hour. Someone stands there blocking the light. Someone has his head split open. Someone walks down Waverly Ave. Someone finds himself used.
>
> This is high tragedy. I will be deformed in hell. (Baraka 49–52)

Twenty-five years later, Derek Walcott reversed the polarity of Baraka's revision of Virgil's and Dante's dream-visions, creating a far more positive blend of earthly scene and Virgilian underworld. Walcott represents himself in *Omeros* returning to his childhood home in the town of Castries on St. Lucia, where he encounters the ghost of his father Warwick, who had died when the poet was a boy. Warwick's shade tells his son of his own childhood memories of women still in a virtual state of slavery, endlessly loading heavy baskets of coal onto steamers for export, "while every hundred-weight basket / was ticked by two tally clerks in their white pith helmets, / and the endless repetition as they climbed the / infernal anthracite hills showed you hell, early" (Walcott 74).

In the *Aeneid*, the ghost of Aeneas's father announces his son's vocation and destiny, which he must pursue upon his return to the upper world: "Roman, remember by your strength to rule / Earth's peoples – for your arts are to be these: / To pacify, to impose the rule of law" (*Aeneid* 6:733–5). Warwick Walcott too confirms his son's destiny, not as a ruler but as a poet:

his art will be art itself. Warwick issues his prophetic command as his son contemplates the laboring women summoned up by his father's memories:

> Kneel to your load, then balance your staggering feet
> and walk up that coal ladder as they do in time,
> one bare foot after the next in ancestral rhyme. (75)

Writing in three-line stanzas recalling Dante's terza rima, Walcott transposes the women's staggering feet into the metrical feet of his verse. "They walk, you write," his father tells him; "your duty / . . . is the chance you now have, to give those feet a voice" (75–6). Transformed across centuries and across oceans, the ancient epic tradition speaks with undiminished power today.

Gathering Rosebuds

So far, we have been following continuities and changes from the distant past up to the present – a logical direction to pursue, as this is how literary history proceeds. For a reader, however, it can also be useful to go backward in time, tracing an image or a scene back to its source or sources. Reading a contemporary writer, we may be struck by a reference to some earlier author, or an editor's footnote may draw our attention to a quotation or a close similarity to a classic character. Sometimes a whole chain of rewritings and borrowings underlies the modern work, and we can plunge downward in time, observing the different tints an image takes on in the glimmering depths of the past.

The process of working backward can be illustrated by exploring the references shown in the foreground of Figure 1, an illustration to a modern translation of Dante's *Inferno* by the British artist Tom Phillips. In this post-modern vision of hell, the dead souls littering the landscape are nothing other than burning books, whose quotations suggest the moral failings that would lead the book – or its reader – to perdition. Prominently displayed in the foreground are two quotations that directly challenge the medieval Christian emphasis on striving for eternal life. On the left is a famous line from the Roman poet Horace, "Carpe diem quam minimum credula postero," "Seize the day, counting little on the morrow." Next to Horace is the first line of a lyric by the Renaissance poet Robert Herrick, "To the Virgins, to Make Much of Time":

Figure 1 Tom Phillips, illustration to Canto X of Dante's *Inferno*, 1983. *Copyright Tom Phillips (DACS)*

Gather ye rosebuds while ye may,
    Old Time is still a-flying:
And this same flower that smiles to-day
    To-morrow will be dying.

The glorious lamp of heaven, the sun,
    The higher he's a-getting,
The sooner will his race be run,
    And nearer he's to setting.

That age is best which is the first,
    When youth and blood are warmer;
But being spent, the worse, and worst
    Times still succeed the former.

Then be not coy, but use your time,
    And while ye may, go marry;
For having lost but once your prime,
    You may for ever tarry.
                (Quiller-Couch 266–7)

The image of gathering rosebuds can be traced back in time from Herrick, for he took his opening line from the conclusion of a famous sonnet by the French poet Pierre Ronsard, who died in 1585, a few years before Herrick was born. One of Ronsard's sonnets to his beloved "Hélène" reads as follows:

Quand vous serez bien vieille, au soir, à la chandelle,
    Assise auprès du feu, devidant et filant,
    Direz, chantant mes vers, et vous esmerveillant:
    Ronsard me celebroit du temps que j'estois belle.
Lors vous n'aurez servante oyant telle nouvelle,
    Desja sous le labeur à demy sommeillant,
    Qui, au bruit de Ronsard, ne s'aille réveillant,
    Benissant vostre nom de louange immortelle.
Je seray sous la terre, et, fantosme sans os,
    Par les ombres myrteux je prendray mon repos;
    Vous serez au fouyer une vieille accroupie,
Regrettant mon amour et vostre fier desdain.
    Vivez, si m'en croyez, n'attendez à demain;
    Cueillez dès aujourd'huy les roses de la vie.
                (Ronsard 1:340)

[When you've reached old age, at night by the candle's flame
  spinning and winding your wool by the fire
  and singing my verses, you'll be moved and declare,
  "Once, when I was lovely, Ronsard gave me fame."
Your serving girls, hearing this phrase
  as they nod, half asleep, over their needlework,
  will rouse themselves at the sound of Ronsard
  blessing your name with immortal praise.
As for me, below ground, a formless shade,
  I'll take my ease in a myrtle glade,
  while at your hearth, hunched over with age,
you'll regret my love and your haughty scorn.
  So live, if you heed me, wait not for the morn:
  Gather in while you can the roses of today.]

Ronsard's lyric is an anguished plea to a particular woman, perhaps a married woman who (in the tradition of French courtly love) disdains to enter into a love affair. Herrick's playful poem has taken the bitter edge from Ronsard's line. He addresses a group of virgins rather than his own beloved and urges them all to marry. This altogether happier scene takes up Christ's parable of the wise and foolish virgins: the wise ones keep their lamps trimmed and don't miss the wedding they're supposed to attend.

  Ronsard's poem, by contrast, is located more squarely within the Epicurean traditions of ancient Rome – in his Dante illustration, Tom Phillips appropriately includes Epicurus among the books in his Inferno. Ronsard's final couplet is a loose translation of Horace's "Carpe diem quam minimum credula postero," bringing out the agricultural implication of the verb "carpe diem." This phrase is often translated as "seize the day," but it could better be rendered as "gather in the day," as though it were a harvest. Ronsard draws also on Horace's contemporary Tibullus (55– c.19 BCE). The brevity of time is a major theme in Tibullus, who died at age thirty-six. In one of his elegies, the dying poet addresses his lover Delia, urging her to be faithful to him even after death:

  But I pray you, continue chaste, your holy modesty
  always preserved, as your aged companion sits beside you.
  She'll tell you tales, the lamp set in its place,
  as she draws out the long yarn from her distaff,
  while all around the girls bend over their needlework
  until sleep overcomes them and the work falls away.

Then may I suddenly appear, unannounced by anyone;
sent down from heaven let me seem to you.
And then to me – just as you are, your tresses disordered,
your feet unsandalled – run, O Delia.
This I pray: may the radiant morning star bless my sight,
borne by the rosy horses of shining Dawn.

(Tibullus, Elegy 1.iii, 83–94)

Ronsard has combined Horace's harvest-gathering image with Tibullus's rosy dawn, building on the situation underlying Tibullus's elegies. The woman called Delia was evidently married to an army officer, and she carried on her affair with Tibullus when her husband was away at war. The dying poet had good reason to be concerned that her mourning might not last so very long; another lover might soon take his place. Yet his tone is intimate and affectionate. He never imagines Delia herself aging; the old woman in the scene is a companion or chaperone. By contrast, Ronsard shows himself in the position of an unrequited lover and combines the beloved girl with the aged crone to striking effect.

There is another and very different source that Ronsard likely drew on, for the theme of gathering rosebuds appears in the Bible, in the apocryphal text known as the Wisdom of Solomon. This book was written by a contemporary of Horace and Tibullus, a Greek-speaking Jew in Alexandria. A strict moralist, the author of the Wisdom of Solomon paints a disapproving picture of the hedonists he sees around him in Egypt:

For they reasoned unsoundly, saying to themselves,
Short and sorrowful is our life,
and there is no remedy when a man comes to his end,
and no one has been known to return from Hades. . . .
. . . . .
Come, therefore, let us enjoy the good things that exist,
and make use of the creation to the full as in youth.
Let us take our fill of costly wine and perfumes,
and let no flower of spring pass by us:
let us crown ourselves with rosebuds before they wither.

(Wisdom of Solomon 2:1, 6–8)

In sharp contrast to the Roman poets, the biblical author is outraged by such Epicureanism. He is concerned not only with personal moral laxity but with its social consequences: he argues that those who live for pleasure will oppress widows and orphans, and will lie in wait for the righteous man "because he is inconvenient to us and opposes our actions" (2:12). For this poet, the brevity of life should be a stimulus to serious reflection and to ethical action in the world. He denies that the godly think only of life after death: "God did not make death, and he does not delight in the death of the living. / . . . For he created all things that they might exist" (1:13–14). It is instead the unrighteous who treat Death as the object of romantic desire: "Ungodly men by their words and deeds summoned Death; / considering him a friend, they pined away, / and they made a covenant with him, / because they are fit to belong to his party" (1:18).

The image of the beloved as a flower in springtime appears positively in the Bible as well: "I am a rose of Sharon, a lily of the valleys," the young woman sings in the Song of Songs, urging her lover to arise and come with her: "for lo, the winter is past, the rain is over and gone, / the flowers appear on the earth, the time of singing has come, / and the voice of the turtledove is heard in our land" (2:1, 11–12). Rather than see such verses as expressing an irreligious hedonism, the rabbis who included it in the Bible chose instead to read the Song of Songs as an allegory of the love of God and Israel. The Church Fathers took up the rabbis' viewpoint, reinterpreting the text as an allegory of the love of Christ and the Church. Dante in turn employed this religiously inflected erotic symbolism, not in his Inferno but in Paradise itself, where the saints circle around God in the form of a radiant celestial rose.

*

The vast landscape of books in Tom Phillips's Inferno extends far back in time, and yet Phillips is a self-consciously modern artist, and his illustration also brings its rosebuds forward from Dante's time to ours. His placing of Herrick in Dante's Inferno involves a deliberate anachronism, as Herrick lived three hundred years after Dante – a good image of the way in which literature reaches beyond its own time. If we look into the distance in Phillips's landscape of open books, we can come closer yet to the present. The farthest books with readable words are a volume of the ancient materialist philosopher-poet Lucretius, and a book whose page says, simply, "ROSEBUD." Phillips's work is filled with references to visual as well as verbal art, and this half-hidden volume evokes the enigmatic last word of Citizen Kane, in the classic film by Orson Welles. The closing shot of *Citizen Kane* reveals that "Rosebud" is not the name of a lost lover, as Kane's listeners believe – and as the entire tradition from Tibullus to Herrick would lead us to suppose. Instead, it is the brand name of Kane's boyhood sled, which Welles uses as a poetic image for the lost innocence of childhood.

In reading back from Herrick and Ronsard to their ancient sources, we gain a fuller sense of the resources on which the later poets drew, and we also see how various "the ancient world" really was. Within a single century, the "carpe diem" motif was used in radically different ways by the biblical and Roman writers, who gather their rosebuds to very different effect. A rose by any other name might smell as sweet, as Shakespeare says, but few flowers have such a rich history – "Les Très Riches Heures de Fleur," in the words of the book that overlaps Phillips's "Rosebud" volume. Gathering them as they may, and using them as they choose, poets and visual artists fashion and refashion the rose into a timeless image of the brevity of time.

Chapter 3

Reading across Cultures

Reading world literature gives us the opportunity to expand our literary and cultural horizons far beyond the boundaries of our own culture. Inspiring as it is, though, the reading of foreign works can pose serious problems. The writer may assume a familiarity with dynasties and divinities we have never heard of; the work is probably in dialogue with a range of previous writers we haven't read; the very form of the work may be strange and hard to assess. A good editor's introduction can clarify a work's historical and literary context, and footnotes can identify unfamiliar names, but there remains the danger that we will find ourselves stuck at the surface of the text, put off by its strangeness or inadvertently making it all too familiar, assimilating it superficially to what we already know. Inevitably, we approach a work with expectations and reading skills shaped by the many works we have read in the past – both those of our home tradition and other foreign works we have already encountered. Rather than trying to erase this fund of prior knowledge, we need to use it productively as our springboard into the new. This chapter will discuss several ways in which we can effectively read new material in comparative perspective, probing similarities and differences that can help us make sense of less familiar works while also illuminating familiar material in new ways.

To be effective, a comparison of disparate works needs to be grounded in some third term or set of concerns that can provide a common basis for analysis. Without some meaningful ground of comparison, we would be left with a scattershot assortment of unrelated works. Bewildered by their sheer variety, we could be reduced to constructing the random connections favored by the literary critics in Jorge Luis Borges's story "Tlön, Uqbar, Orbis Tertius." Tlön's critics believe that all literature expresses a hidden unity, and they "will take two dissimilar works – the *Tao Te Ching* and the *1001 Nights*, for instance – attribute them to a single author, and then in all good conscience determine the psychology of that most interesting *homme de lettres*" (Borges, *Collected Fictions* 77).

Fortunately, we are not forced to rely on random free association when dealing with works from unrelated cultures. Distant writers may not share a common fund of literary reference or poetic technique, yet there are many ways to compare works from different cultures. Using the example of drama, this chapter will discuss modes of comparison involving similarities in genre, in character and plot, in themes and imagery, and in parallel cultural patterns or social settings. Together, these examples will illustrate effective strategies for relating works from distant cultures.

Classical Drama: Greece and India

A basic ground of comparison of works from different cultures is provided by literary genres, which play a major role in the shaping of works and in forming audiences' expectations for them. While some genres are unique to a single tradition, others can be found in many parts of the globe; the previous chapter's discussion of epic within the Western tradition could be extended across cultures to look at epics from India, Persia, and North Africa. Drama is still more widespread, found in many cultures at many times. Though the world's different dramatic traditions vary widely, they collectively explore the possibilities opened up by staged performance – the embodiment of characters and actions, the use of props and scenery, the incorporation of music, dance, and lighting. Within these overall parameters, we can learn a good deal about a culture by seeing which elements a given tradition highlights, and how its writers use them. Conversely, a culture's overall dramatic norms provide a crucial starting point for understanding the workings of a particular play – including the playwright's departures from the reigning norms of the day.

We will begin by looking at two masterpieces of world drama: Sophocles' *Oedipus the King* and Kalidasa's *Shakuntala*. Sophocles and Kalidasa have comparable standing as foundational dramatists in their respective traditions, but there is little traceable relation between the drama of Greece and India. Hellenistic kings did rule northern India in the final centuries BCE, and the remains of a Greek theater of this period have been uncovered in what is now Afghanistan. Any such contacts, however, lay in the distant past by Kalidasa's day in the fourth or fifth century, and Sanskrit drama developed on its own terms over many centuries, drawing for its material on Indian epic and lyric traditions rather than on any foreign material. Kalidasa would never have heard of Sophocles, and yet for all their differences, *Shakuntala* and *Oedipus* are comparable on several levels, starting with their fundamental themes.

Sophocles' play is a drama of knowledge. Faced with a plague and blight devastating his city of Thebes, Oedipus seeks to discover what crime or fault has led the gods to punish Thebes in this way. He is resolute in seeking out witnesses who may be able to provide clues, and he progressively teases out the truth. Early on, an oracle reveals that the gods are trying to force Thebes to expel a murderer in their midst, the unknown slayer of Thebes' previous king, Laius. Oedipus then vows to get to the bottom of this crime and to banish the murderer, whoever he may be. What he doesn't realize is that he himself is the murderer in question. While some playwrights might have saved this revelation for the conclusion, Sophocles brings it forward early in the drama, when the blind prophet Teiresias shocks Oedipus by declaring that "you are the land's pollution. / . . . you are the murderer of the king / whose murderer you seek" (Sophocles 101). Worse still, the murdered king Laius, unknown to Oedipus, was actually his own father, who had abandoned him in infancy, hoping to avert a prophecy that he would be slain by his son. Having unwittingly fulfilled this prophecy, Oedipus became Thebes' king and married Laius' widow, Jocasta – his own mother.

The balance of the play concerns Oedipus's efforts to prove or disprove the truth of this horrifying and incredible news. The play is tightly focused on Oedipus and his immediate circle as they grapple with their situation, their characters revealed by their strategies of denial or acceptance. The entire play takes place in a single location and on a single day, effectively in real time, as actions of the distant past come inexorably to light. Long-forgotten or repressed events culminate in a tragic hour of reversals and recognitions, bringing a great man from the height of good fortune to the depths of despair and disgrace. Mediating between the characters and the audience, a chorus of Thebans performs moving laments, singing as they dance.

Kalidasa's *Shakuntala* also involves a great king who has to grapple with a wrong that he has committed at some point in a forgotten past. Like Sophocles, Kalidasa is dramatizing an incident handed down in epic tradition, in his case the Indian epic *Mahabharata*. Hunting one day in a forest, King Dushyanta happens upon a hermitage where he espies the radiantly beautiful Shakuntala, an orphan who is being raised by an ascetic sage. Instantly, Dushyanta falls in love with Shakuntala, and the feeling is reciprocated as soon as she sees the lordly monarch. The two consummate a private marriage, and Dushyanta gives Shakuntala his signet ring and then returns to his court, promising to send shortly for her to join him as his principal wife.

Trouble emerges, however, in the form of an angry spirit named Durvasas, who becomes enraged when Shakuntala fails to greet him with respect (her thoughts are elsewhere as she dreams of her lover). He delivers a curse, repaying her absentmindedness by decreeing that King Dushyanta will forget he ever knew her. Implored by Shakuntala's companions to lift this curse, Durvasas relents to the extent of allowing that Dushyanta will recall his love if he once again sees his signet ring. This, however, slips from Shakuntala's finger as she bathes in a river while traveling to the king's court. When she is presented to Dushyanta, the bewildered king insists he has no recollection of ever having met her, much less married her. Shakuntala – already pregnant from their few days together in the forest – is devastated that she can do nothing to restore his memory. Her own foster-family doubts her story, and disowns her. Angelic forces whisk her away to a Himalayan paradise, where she gives birth to their son and begins to raise him.

All is not lost, however, for a fisherman finds the lost ring, and is brought to the king to explain how he got it. Seeing the ring, Dushyanta immediately remembers everything; he longs to recover Shakuntala but cannot find where the gods have taken her. The situation is finally rectified several years later, when the chief god Indra commissions Dushyanta to defeat an army of demons. After he does so, Indra rewards Dushyanta by having him flown to the Himalayan peak where Shakuntala is living; they are joyfully reunited and Dushyanta meets his son and heir for the first time. The play ends with the happy family mounting Indra's chariot to fly home.

Though comic rather than tragic in mode, *Shakuntala* is as much a psychological drama as *Oedipus the King*. Like Oedipus, Dushyanta is haunted by memories he can't quite bring to consciousness, and he too struggles to make sense of an incredible story: that he has met and married the most beautiful woman in the world and yet has forgotten her within a space of days. After he has returned to his court but before Shakuntala appears, the amnesiac Dushyanta hears one of his wives singing a song of abandonment, and finds himself overcome. "Why did hearing that song's words fill me with such strong desire?" he asks himself; "I'm not parted from anyone I love." He is moved to put his confusion into verse:

> Seeing rare beauty,
> hearing lovely sounds,
> even a happy man
> becomes strangely uneasy. . . .
> perhaps he remembers,
> without knowing why,
> loves of another life
> buried deep in his being.
> (Kalidasa 134)

Sigmund Freud used Oedipus to illustrate the workings of subconscious desires; here Dushyanta is equally troubled by a memory lingering just below the surface of his consciousness. The happy ending in the seventh act is preceded by three full acts of bewilderment, confusion, and heartbreak. In the fourth act, Shakuntala and her companions at the hermitage are dismayed that no messages have come from Dushyanta to invite her to his court. Finally her foster-father Kanva determines to send her anyway, though he is full of sorrow at losing her, as well as of foreboding concerning her reception at court. In the fifth act, Shakuntala and her companions are shocked at Dushyanta's calm refusal to admit to the marriage. "Ascetics," the baffled king says to her guides, "even though I'm searching my mind, I don't remember marrying this lady. How can I accept a woman who is visibly pregnant when I doubt that I am the cause?" (139). Shakuntala is overwhelmed with shame and regret for ever having fallen in love with this seemingly faithless man. Until the play's final act, she is caught in a tragic situation, accused of sinful sexual behavior within the holy precincts of Kanva's hermitage, condemned like Oedipus to be an outcast from society.

Patterns of imagery reinforce the plays' similarities in character and plot. Drama is an eminently visual medium, and like many reflective playwrights after them, Sophocles and Kalidasa incorporate their medium's features among their own themes. In both plays, the characters talk a great deal about what they can and can't see. Oedipus and the blind prophet Teiresias trade accusations about which of them is more blind, and as Oedipus begins to realize the terrible truth of the prophet's charge, he cries out, "I have a deadly fear / that the old seer had eyes" (120). Oedipus constantly casts his quest for knowledge in visual terms: a messenger's "face is bright . . . his news too may be bright for us"; "I wish to see this shepherd" (121, 89). Sight becomes the embodiment of insight, and at the play's end Oedipus famously, gruesomely turns his wrath on his own eyes.

Sight yields insight in *Shakuntala* as well. Throughout the play, people closely watch what other people are doing, and they often comment on the act of seeing itself. When Dushyanta flies through the air in Indra's chariot, this journey is conveyed to the audience not through special effects but by having the king and his charioteer discuss the marvels they see far below them. In Act 3, eager to learn more about Shakuntala, Dushyanta follows her track, analyzing the visual evidence like some love-smitten Sherlock:

> I see fresh footprints
> on white sand in the clearing,
> deeply pressed at the heel
> by the sway of full hips.
> I'll just look through the branches. (112)

He then describes what he (but not the audience) can see: Shakuntala's two female companions massaging her breasts with lotus lotion as they try to cure her lovesickness, which they mistake for heat exhaustion. Dushyanta rejoices in the sight: "My eyes," he declares, "have found bliss!" (112).

Following his first conversation with Shakuntala, Dushyanta surmises her love for him from clues picked up by observing her eyes, mouth, and movements: "Her eyes were cast down in my presence," he reflects, "but she found an excuse to smile. . . . When we parted, her feelings for me showed despite her modesty." He shifts into verse as he ponders the evidence he has acquired:

> "A blade of kuśa grass
> pricked my foot,"
> the girl said for no reason
> after walking a few steps away;
> then she pretended to free
> her bark dress from the branches
> where it was not caught
> and shyly glanced at me. (107)

Like Oedipus, Dushyanta prides himself on being all-seeing and all knowing; having rejected Shakuntala under the spell of amnesia, he too must suffer the realization of his tragic error. This realization is precipitated by the sight of his signet ring brought by the fisherman – a combined moment of recognition and reversal, the pairing of elements that Aristotle praises in the *Poetics*, singling out this pairing in *Oedipus* as the height of dramatic art.

Tragic Flaw or Fate?

Oedipus and *Shakuntala* are products of ancient, polytheistic societies, in which numbers of gods were believed to act in all areas of earthly life. Reading *Shakuntala* along with *Oedipus* can help us see how both playwrights held very different assumptions from most of their modern successors. From the Renaissance onward, Western dramatists focused their attention on individual character and judgment, and tragic heroes were understood in terms of the tragic flaws that had brought them down. The classical Greek plays came to be read in terms of such flaws as overweening pride or hubris, an emphasis more in tune with later Christian values than with those of the ancient Greeks. Aristotle valued plot over character, and argued that a true tragic hero must in fact be a good and even great man; the downfall of someone bad would be something good, not a tragedy at all. As for pride, it reflected a hero's just sense of his abilities. Certainly Oedipus is proud of his ability to govern his city, solve riddles, and control his destiny, and this pride is humbled by the play's end. Yet Sophocles is equally, even primarily, concerned to show the overpowering role of destiny in the course of human affairs. The infant Oedipus was in no way responsible for bringing down the curse that would destroy him decades later. Instead, he was wrong to think he could avert the fate decreed by the gods, and the play relentlessly takes apart Oedipus's confident belief that he can save the day by his detective work. In an implicit rebuke to his fellow Athenians' growing reliance on reason as the means to command their own destiny, Sophocles shows that even the greatest hero can be brought down by the will of the gods.

In his emphasis on fate over individual ability, Sophocles is closer to Kalidasa than to many later dramatists in the West. Shakuntala's curse has more to do with the irascibility of the spirit Durvasas than with any moral failing on her part, and the curse brings equal suffering to Dushyanta, who was nowhere near the forest when Durvasas went into his

52

sudden fit of rage. The curse of forgetfulness prevents him from solving a problem he never knew about in the first place. Indeed, he and Shakuntala had little or no choice in falling in love to begin with. Love at first sight is a common theme in Western romantic tradition, but Kalidasa goes Hollywood one better: his hero experiences love *before* first sight. Merely approaching Shakuntala's forest glen, Dushyanta feels a suggestive trembling in his muscles:

> The hermitage is a tranquil place,
> yet my arm is quivering . . .
> do I feel a false omen of love,
> or does fate have doors everywhere? (93)

Oedipus and Dushyanta are exemplary rulers, taken by surprise by their fate. In each play, the emphasis is on seeing how the characters handle the predicament into which they find themselves thrust. Both rulers must come to accept their destiny, as their attempts to avoid it only make things worse.

When he falls in love, Dushyanta hides his love from his companions, preferring to consummate a marriage in secret and then return home to prepare the way for Shakuntala's eventual arrival. If Dushyanta had admitted the relationship openly, at whatever cost to his existing marriages and political alliances, Shakuntala would never have been left alone to pine away for him in the forest, and the issue of the curse would never have arisen. Later, while suffering his amnesia Dushyanta refuses to take Shakuntala as his bride, even though he is deeply attracted to her, because he refuses to steal another man's mistress, as he insists the pregnant Shakuntala must be. His virtuous response actually compounds the problem, much as Oedipus only makes things worse by his best efforts to flee the curse on his family and then to find the king's murderer.

Oedipus, Dushyanta, and Shakuntala show their true worth in their ultimate response to their situation. Having been rejected by her husband and her family alike, Shakuntala maintains the truth but refuses to stay in the king's household as a dishonored hanger-on. She raises her son in exile, never giving way to despair, and she is able to embrace the joyful resolution at the play's end. As for Dushyanta, having realized his error in rejecting Shakuntala, he mourns her loyally for years, while also continuing to perform his royal duties: he thus atones for his actions (as a companion declares) even though they were hardly his own fault. Oedipus

53

too rises to the challenge of his fate. Whereas his wife Jocasta proceeds from obstruction of Oedipus's quest to suicidal despair once the truth can no longer be denied, Oedipus moves beyond an initial, paranoid insistence that the prophet Teiresias must be corrupt, in league with his brother-in-law Creon; he persists in seeking the truth, even as he increasingly realizes it will mean his own ruin. Though he inflicts blindness upon himself at the play's end, he rejects suicide, accepting his fate and preparing to let it take him where it will. In many ways, Oedipus resembles Dushyanta more than he resembles Shakespeare's King Lear or Mozart's Don Giovanni, brought down chiefly by their own flaws.

Character and Plot

Though there are fascinating similarities between *Oedipus* and *Shakuntala* on several levels, we should not ignore the noteworthy differences between the plays. Indeed, these differences become as interesting as the similarities, revealing important divergences in each dramatist's methods and in the expectations of their audiences. The differences start to be apparent as early as the opening list of the cast of characters. Typically for Greek plays, *Oedipus* has a limited number of parts. Most of the play's scenes involve Oedipus in dialogue with only one other person: his wife, his brother-in-law, or a series of minor characters who each appear in a single scene: the prophet Teiresias, a priest, two messengers, and a herdsman. Apart from the chorus, there are never more than three speakers on stage at once, and Sophocles was already stretching the cast by introducing a third actor, as two had been the norm before him. Greek actors used masks, so they could switch roles simply by changing their mask, and the Chorus itself always speaks as "I" and could at a minimum be played by a single person.

Kalidasa's stage is far more crowded than its Greek counterpart. Whereas *Oedipus* has a total of eight speaking roles, *Shakuntala* has no fewer than forty-four, not counting assorted spirits who are heard as offstage voices. Shakuntala and Dushyanta are constantly surrounded by friends, relations, and courtiers, in keeping with the densely populated social world of Indian lyric poetry discussed in Chapter 1. Even the scenes in the isolated forest hermitage involve more speakers than appear in the center of Thebes during the entire span of *Oedipus the King*. Kalidasa's larger cast takes part in a more episodic plot than is found in the Greek drama, with its characteristic unities of time, place, and action. *Shakuntala*'s seven acts span a period of several years – enough time for Shakuntala to meet and marry Dushyanta, give birth to their son, and then raise him beyond infancy; when we see them in the final act, the bold boy is playing with a lion cub in preference to his toys.

The larger cast and greater time span of the Sanskrit drama do not mean, though, that action plays a greater role than in *Oedipus*. Where *Oedipus* is a drama of knowledge centered on the detection of a hidden crime and a repressed curse, *Shakuntala* is a drama of sentiment and lyrical reflection. Lyricism has its place in Sophocles as well, embodied in the Chorus with its strophic hymns and dance. In Kalidasa, it is the major characters who continually break into song or pause for poetic reverie. Even the mighty king Dushyanta is a meditative poet as well as a man of action. Many of his speeches take the form of a declarative sentence followed by a poem in which he reflects on the situation in general terms:

> This bark dress fits her body badly, but it ornaments her beauty . . .
>> A tangle of duckweed adorns a lotus,
>> a dark spot heightens the moon's glow,
>> the bark dress increases her charm –
>> beauty finds its ornaments anywhere. (95)

In keeping with this lyrical emphasis, *Shakuntala* leaves its major actions offstage. Shakuntala and Dushyanta feel the stirrings of love in the first act, then in the second act the king thinks at length about his newfound passion but doesn't act upon it. The lovers admit their mutual devotion in the third act, but they don't even have a chance to kiss, as the king is called away to perform rituals at the hermitage shrine. Their wedding evidently occurs between acts. When the fourth act opens, Dushyanta is already back at court; Shakuntala is pregnant and pining away – exquisitely – for her departed lover. Later, the heartrending confrontation of the amnesiac king and his forgotten bride is fully staged, but we are not shown the crucial recognition scene, in which Dushyanta sees the ring and remembers all – we only hear about it, after the fact, in a brief speech between two minor characters.

Kalidasa's plot serves as a frame for a succession of pantomimes, dances, and songs, which delicately unfold the characters' responses to their experiences. With the essence of poetry taken to be found in echoes, overtones, nuances, and hints, India's playwrights too preferred to emphasize the expression of emotion over dramatic action. The downplaying of action represents a significant difference from much Western drama, though there is again less contrast between Kalidasa and Sophocles than with later Western playwrights. Sophocles too leaves major plot events offstage – not only the early history of the curse on Oedipus's parents but also the climax of the action at the play's end: Jocasta's suicide and Oedipus's self-mutilation. As in Kalidasa, these crucial events are described secondhand by minor characters. Even so, the descriptions in *Oedipus* become lush with bloody detail: "the bleeding eyeballs gushed / and stained his beard – no sluggish oozing drops / but a black rain and bloody hail poured down" (143). Almost more vivid than an actual enactment would have been, such reports gave the playwright a way to portray shocking events even when propriety dictated that they should not be put on stage.*(Our word "obscene" comes from the Greek term *ob-skēnē*, "off-stage.") The brief summaries of off-stage events given in *Shakuntala* have nothing like this dramatic effect.

Later European drama began to put more "obscene" material onstage. *King Lear* puts out Gloucester's eyes before our own eyes: "Out, vile jelly!" he grimly declares as he does so. When Othello strangles Desdemona, the stage lights stay on as he declares that he will put out her light, and *Hamlet* reaches its bloody climax with a whole series of onstage stabbings and poisonings. If we have grown up with Shakespeare – not to mention the sexual display and violence of contemporary cinema and television – we need to adjust our expectations when reading Sophocles as well as Kalidasa, entering a different rhythm and literary space, a world of suggestive indirection rather than of dramatic action.

Scenes from Middle-class Life

Our examination of Sophocles and Kalidasa has centered on similarities in character and plot, but it is also illuminating to compare works in terms of their representation of social life. Age-old patterns can serve as a backdrop for artistic work, as was the case with monarchy and polytheism in *Oedipus* and *Shakuntala*, but works can also take account of new phenomena such as changing social relations or new political orders. One such upheaval was the rise to prominence of the commercial middle class in regions of the world formerly dominated by a feudal aristocracy. In more than one part of the world the merchant class began to make itself heard with new force during the seventeenth and eighteenth centuries, decisively displacing the older aristocracy during the nineteenth century. Literary works began to treat this shift during its first phases, and fascinating comparisons can be made among works from very different cultures that were undergoing their own versions of this process.

As a case in point, we will look at *Le Bourgeois Gentilhomme* (1670) by the French playwright Molière, and *Love Suicides at Amijima* (1721) by Chikamatsu Mon'zaemon, the greatest Japanese dramatist of the period. These playwrights were close contemporaries; Chikamatsu was twenty years old when Molière died. Though the French and Japanese theatrical traditions were completely independent of each other and varied in fundamental ways, in these plays both dramatists were thinking hard about the new social order that was starting to come into being around them. This common concern yields fascinating convergences – as well as equally interesting divergences – between their works.

Molière's title is intended as a paradox: a middle-class merchant was not supposed to be a gentleman. The term *gentilhomme* had originated in the Middle Ages to signify someone born within the extended circle of the nobility. Molière's Monsieur Jourdain, however, has deluded himself into thinking he can vault into the upper class by mere virtue of the wealth he has inherited from his father, a prosperous cloth merchant. He is embarrassed by his modest origins, and rejoices at the flattery of a servant who pretends that Jourdain's father had been a kind of connoisseur of cloth, not a merchant at all:

> M. JOURDAIN: There are foolish people about who will have it that my father was in trade.
>
> COVEILLE: In trade! Sheer slander! Never in his life! It was just that he was obliging, anxious to be helpful, and as he knew all about cloth he would go round and select samples, have them brought to his house and give them to his friends – for a consideration. (Molière 50)

Monsieur Jourdain knows, though, that to become a *gentilhomme* he must do more than cover up his origins: he needs education, refinement, and aristocratic tastes. So he has hired a dancing master, a music teacher, a fencing coach, and even a philosopher to give him all the cultural advantages a true gentleman should enjoy. The play opens with the music teacher and the dancing master arguing whether Jourdain's lavish payments make up for the indignity of teaching him; though the dancing master is embarrassed to have such an uncultured client, the music teacher gladly puts up with Jourdain, for "his praise has cash value" (4).

In this world of trade and exchange, Jourdain isn't content to trade up only in matters of taste. He insists that his daughter must marry a nobleman, and he personally hopes to enjoy the sexual license for which the French aristocracy was notorious. Though he has a wife of his own modest background, he is deeply in love – or so he claims – with Countess Dorimène, a woman so far above his station in life that he's never managed to have a conversation with her. He does, however, enjoy the friendship of a dissolute nobleman named Dorante, whose name could be translated "Golden" or "Glittering." Dorante continually bleeds Jourdain for money to pay off tradesmen and to advance his own romance with Dorimène herself: he has been pretending to plead Jourdain's case with her, though in reality he has been passing along Jourdain's lavish presents as though they were his own.

A world away, Chikamatsu explored similar social tensions in *Love Suicides at Amijima*. His hero, Jihei, is a paper merchant; as the chanter who narrates the action says approvingly, "The paper is honestly sold, and the shop is well situated; it is a long-established firm, and the customers come thick as raindrops" (Chikamatsu 403). Like Jourdain, Jihei is married to a woman from his own walk of life, but he has fallen in love with someone above his means: Koharu, a high-class prostitute, whose clients include samurai and other members of the nobility. Koharu has returned his love, and Jihei is desperate to buy her out of her brothel, but he has nothing like the money needed for the purpose. His romantic rival, a wealthy merchant named Tahei, is sure that money is all he needs to win Koharu: "when it comes to money, I'm an easy winner. If I pushed with all the strength of my money, who knows what I might conquer?" He believes that commerce has supplanted age-old social relations: "A customer's a customer," he says, "whether he's a samurai or a townsman. The only difference is that one wears swords and the other doesn't" (392).

In Japan as in France, clothing was a powerful marker of social status, and both Molière and Chikamatsu portray characters trying to adopt a new social role by donning a new costume. Monsieur Jourdain is obsessed with the extravagant, ill-fitting clothes his tailor foists off on him as the latest fashion among the nobility; he is discomfited that his wife and her maid can't stop laughing when they see him in his ridiculous plumes and ruffles. In *Love Suicides at Amijima*, Jihei dresses up to impress the proprietress of the brothel when he goes to buy Koharu's freedom, but on his way he is confronted by his angry father-in-law, who accuses Jihei of seeking to disguise his humble origins: "My esteemed son-in-law," he says sarcastically, "what a rare pleasure to see you dressed in your finest attire, with a dirk and a silken cloak! Ahhh – that's how a gentleman of means spends his money! No one would take you for a paper dealer" (411).

Both plays include speeches describing the act of dressing up as a form of play-acting. Molière's Monsieur Jourdain has refused to allow his daughter to marry her true love, Cléonte, because he isn't a nobleman, but Cléonte's clever servant Coveille solves the problem by proposing "an idea I got from a play I saw some time ago" (42). He dresses his master up as a Turkish prince, and Jourdain is only too happy to accept this exotic nobleman as his son-in-law. The disguised Cléonte bestows upon Jourdain a fake title, "Mamamouchi" (vaguely derived from "Mameluke," an Ottoman military caste). Cléonte then costumes Jourdain in Turkish finery, prompting Jourdain's astonished daughter to exclaim: "Is this a play?"

Far more seriously, in *Love Suicides at Amijima* Jihei and Koharu have realized that they can never be free in their love, and they are planning to commit suicide. Desperately trying to prevent some such rash act, Jihei's brother Magoemon dresses up as a samurai and comes to Koharu in the guise of a customer, using the authority of his assumed upper-class rank to add weight to his words as he tries to dissuade her from throwing her life away. Magoemon feels like an actor in his samurai outfit: "Here I am," he grumbles, "dressed up like a masquerader at a festival or maybe a lunatic! I put on swords for the first time in my life and announced myself, like a bit player in a costume piece" (401).

In both plays, traditional social norms assert themselves beneath the new roles. The vulgar Tahei claims that samurai and commoners are all just customers, yet he retreats from the brothel in awe when confronted with a genuine samurai – in actual fact, Jihei's brother in samurai disguise (393). Monsieur Jourdain believes that clothes make the nobleman, but he can never fool anyone, partly because he hasn't even inherited enough skill from his cloth merchant father to know what an upper-class outfit should look like. Both Jihei and Jourdain find their love lives sharply constrained by their wives' refusal to play along. Jihei's wife, Osan, is counseled by her aunt, who declares that "A man's dissipation can always be traced to his wife's carelessness. . . . You'd do well to take notice of what's going on and assert yourself a bit more" (405). Osan confronts Jihei and even writes a letter of appeal to Koharu, puncturing their dream of simple togetherness. As the play proceeds, though, Osan comes to a deeper understanding of her husband's bond with Koharu, and in an exceptional gesture of solidarity with both of them, Osan pawns her own clothing to help Jihei scrape together the money to buy Koharu's freedom. Jihei then dresses in his finest clothing to go and effect the ransom, only to have his disastrous encounter with his father-in-law, who refuses to countenance any understanding between Jihei, Osan, and Koharu. The lovers choose suicide as their only way out of their unbearable situation.

In Molière's comedy, society's norms are asserted far more positively against the protagonist's wishes – a happy result even for Monsieur Jourdain, who never had any chance with Dorimène to begin with. Jourdain's wife breaks up a dinner party he has arranged for Dorimène and Dorante; "I stand for my rights," she tells her husband, "and every wife will be on my side" (49). Like Jihei's wife, she confronts her rival directly: "as for you, madam, it ill becomes a fine lady to be causing trouble in a decent family and letting my husband think he's in love with you" (48). This charge puzzles Dorimène, who has only just met Jourdain and believes that he is merely providing a convenient place for her to meet her suitor Dorante. She no more approves of crossing class boundaries than does Jourdain's wife, who asserts that "marrying above one's station always brings trouble" (41).

Molière and Chikamatsu both explored the stirrings of a new class mobility, using their own profession, acting, as a powerful metaphor for life in a world of unstable social identities. Yet the differences between their plays are considerable as well, not only because of broad cultural differences but equally as a result of the personal choices the two playwrights had made in their own lives. Molière had come from the very merchant class he satirizes in his play. His father had been a wealthy upholsterer who had built on his connections to his noble clientele to promote himself and his family into a tenuous position within court circles – just the ambition of the cloth dealer's son Jourdain, whom Molière actually played in the play's premiere. Distancing himself from his roots even as he drew on them, Molière wrote *Le Bourgeois Gentilhomme* as a farce to entertain the court of Louis XIV; the serious tensions of class upheaval motivate the drama but are cast in a ridiculous light.

By contrast, *Love Suicides at Amijima* is a heart-rending tragedy, one of two dozen plays that Chikamatsu wrote about commoner life. Throughout the play, the middle-class characters reveal depths of emotion and painful sensitivity that bourgeois characters rarely exhibit in Molière or indeed in most European drama of the day. The intense emotionality of Chikamatsu's characters is particularly impressive as they aren't embodied by human actors at all, for <u>*Love Suicides at Amijima* is a puppet play</u>. Chikamatsu had moved in the opposite social direction from Molière in establishing himself as his century's greatest master of the puppet theater. Born into a wealthy family of the samurai class, he had served in aristocratic house-holds as a youth, but then had left the capital of Kyoto and moved to Osaka, center of the growing class of commoner merchants. There he became involved in the popular entertainment form of the puppet theater, full of colorful incidents and rollicking action. <u>Chikamatsu helped develop puppetry into a remarkably fluid and intense form of art, with the puppets bought to life by solemn puppeteers as a narrator described their fleeting joys and lasting griefs, endowing the puppets with all the nuances of human emotion.</u>

Watching Koharu through her latticed window as she entertains a customer, Jihei "beckons to her with his heart, his spirit flies to her," the narrator says; "but his body, like a cicada's cast-off shell, clings to the lattice-work. He weeps with impatience" (396). As Jihei helps Koharu slip away from the brothel to consummate their suicide pact, ~~the simple~~ opening of the door becomes a scene of agonizing suspense:

> She is all impatience, but the more quickly they open the door, the more likely people will be to hear the casters turning. They lift the door; it makes a moaning sound that thunders in their ears and in their hearts. Jihei lends a hand from the outside, but his fingertips tremble with the trembling of his heart. The door opens a quarter of an inch, a half, an inch – <u>an inch ahead are the tortures of hell, but more than hell itself they fear the guardian-demon's eyes.</u> (418)

Finally they make their escape, and the narrator sorrowfully chants their progress toward their chosen place of death: "The frost now falling will melt by dawn, but even more quickly than this symbol of human frailty, the lovers themselves will melt away. What will become of the fragrance that lingered when he held her tenderly at night in their bedchamber?" (418).

Chikamatsu's world is both intensely realistic and freighted with poetic symbolism. In the play's final act, the doomed lovers cross a series of bridges with names such as Onari, "Becoming a Buddha." Whereas in a European play we would expect religious symbolism to stand on the side of the sacrament of marriage, <u>Chikamatsu shows his hero and heroine progressing together to spiritual enlightenment at the play's end.</u> Just before committing suicide, they cut off their hair, renouncing the world as if they are a monk and a nun; but they look forward to being reborn together in the future. As Koharu says, "What have we to grieve about? Although in this world we could not stay together, in the next and through each successive world to come until the end of time we shall be husband and wife." Koharu has made this expectation a centerpiece of her religious practice: "Every summer for my devotions I have copied the All Compassionate and All Merciful Chapter of the Lotus Sutra, in the hope that we may be reborn on one lotus" (420).

By infusing his play with such deep poetic and philosophical elements, Chikamatsu built a bridge of his own: between the rough-and-tumble world of the puppet play and the meditative, refined aristocratic art with which he had grown up. Like Chikamatsu, Molière made his mark by revolutionizing what had been a simpler, popular dramatic form: stage farce up to his day had consisted largely of buffoonery, with stock characters played for broad humor by actors in colorful masks – human puppets, we might say. If Chikamatsu brought an aristocratic sensibility to the world of popular entertainment, Molière brought a down-to-earth realism to his portrayal of the aristocratic world. Though he wrote his play for the court, his portrayal of courtly life is hardly flattering: Dorimène is a cynic, and Dorante is a lying, manipulative creep. There can be little doubt that their marriage will be an endless series of intrigues and bad debts. The characters who are destined for happiness at the play's end are the plain-spoken Cléonte and Jourdain's lively, loving daughter Lucile – played by Molière's wife at the play's premiere. The future belongs to them, rather than to the aristocracy that Jourdain impossibly hopes to join.

From Oedipus to Elesin

A fruitful basis for reading across cultures is often the comparison of two works that resonate with and against each other on several levels, as in the pairings discussed above. As we build up a fund of reading, we can also triangulate among a variety of works, reading across several eras and cultures at once as we find different works that relate to different aspects of a text. To take one example, Wole Soyinka's *Death and the King's Horseman* (1975) combines many literary strands as it dramatizes multiple conflicts: between cultures, generations, and the sexes, and between contradictory impulses in its hero's heart. The play is based on an event that occurred in Nigeria in 1946, when a Yoruba king died and the Horseman of the King prepared to commit suicide, as commanded by tradition, in order to accompany his king into the afterlife. Nigeria was then a British colony, and the colonial District Officer placed the horseman under arrest in order to prevent the ritual suicide from taking place – an act of mercy that backfired when the horseman's eldest son committed suicide in his father's place.

In staging this story, Soyinka drew extensively on traditional Yoruba drama, in which music, song, and dance convey much of a work's meaning. In its dramaturgy, *Death and the King's Horseman* can be compared with *Shakuntala*; Soyinka's tragic hero, Elesin, is as eloquent a poet as Kalidasa's King Dushyanta, and his powerful songs and dances dominate several of the play's key scenes as he prepares to lay down his life. Soyinka also draws on the traditions of Greek tragedy; two years before completing his play, indeed, he had published an adaptation of Euripides, *The Bacchae: A Communion Rite.* Oedipus and Elesin are each faced with the need to carry through an ancestral pattern that some in the play – Jocasta in Sophocles, District Officer Pilkings in Soyinka – wish to relegate to ancient history. In both plays, however, the life of the community requires the hero's self-sacrifice. *Death and the King's Horseman* also ends with a Sophoclean combination of reversal and recognition, complete with dialogue concerning vision and blindness: when Elesin's son discovers that his father has not succeeded in committing suicide as he should, Elesin reacts to his son's palpable disgust by crying, "Oh son, don't let the sight of your father turn you blind!" (Soyinka 49). The son's blinding insight into his father's failure is then doubled with the father's reciprocal vision of his son' success, when his son's body is displayed to him in the final scene.

Soyinka's play can also be compared to Shakespeare's dramas. In five-act Shakespearean form, *Death and the King's Horseman* builds to a dramatic climax when Elesin, confronted with his son's corpse, shocks his captors by strangling himself with his own chains – the kind of violent incident that Kalidasa and Sophocles would have kept offstage. Soyinka also resembles Shakespeare and later dramatists in the emphasis given to the hero's internal contradictions: Elesin has delayed his suicide in order to consummate a last-minute marriage, unable fully to free himself from earthly attachments as he should. Elesin can be seen as embodying a modern tragic hero's fatal flaw of pride.

Yet his story is also the tragedy of a community struggling to uphold its traditions in the face of colonial domination, in ways comparable to the influential novel *Things Fall Apart* by Soyinka's friend Chinua Achebe, as well as to many other works of colonial and postcolonial drama and fiction written elsewhere. Elesin's downfall comes about not only through his own pride, but also through the interference of District Officer Pilkings, who thinks he knows what is best for Elesin and tries to save him from himself. As a wise woman, Iyaloja, tells Pilkings at the play's end as they stand over the bodies of Elesin and his son: "The gods demanded only the old expired plantain but you cut down the sap-laden shoot to feed your pride" (62). Iyaloja is a voice for her community's collective experience, and in shaping her character Soyinka has drawn not only on traditional Yoruba and classical Greek traditions but also on such modern tragedians as Bertolt Brecht and Eugene O'Neill. Iyaloja inherits qualities from Brecht's Mother Courage as well as from O'Neill's Electra.

Taken together, Sophocles, Kalidasa, Molière, Chikamatsu, and Soyinka can suggest the different levels on which we can compare works from distant traditions, in terms of theme, imagery, character, plot, or broader social and cultural concerns. Once established, a productive comparison will suggest many further avenues to pursue. Deeper examination of these works would reveal new levels of difference and of similarity, and further reading in the literature of each culture can greatly deepen our understanding of these varied levels. New juxtapositions will open up over time as we read further: Shakuntala and Dushyanta could be compared, for instance, to Viola and Count Orsino in Shakespeare's *Twelfth Night*, struggling to fathom an attraction that defies the evidence of their senses. We can find Sophocles's Oedipus ironically re-created as a young woman, Oedipa Maas, in Thomas Pynchon's novel *The Crying of Lot 49* – a book very much concerned with hidden, fatal patterns. Love leads to suicide for Flaubert's Madame Bovary and Tolstoy's Anna Karenina, whose tragedies could be compared in various ways to that of Chikamatsu's Jihei and Koharu. Like the suicides of Elesin and his son, their double suicide represents an ambiguous redemption of age-old passions amid the tensions of a new modern world. As we cross the boundaries between their worlds and the wider worlds before, after, and around them, we can see new facets of *Death and the King's Horseman* each time it is staged, and find new possibilities for Koharu and Jihei each time they are reborn on their lotus leaf.

Chapter 4

Reading in Translation

Most literature circulates in the world in translation. Even languages of global reach, such as English, Spanish, and Arabic, are spoken only by a minority of the world's readers. The power of global English is marked in part by the speed with which popular authors such as Stephen King and J. K. Rowling are translated into dozens of languages, while the importance of translation is even more pronounced for works in less widely spoken languages. Without translation, the novelist Orhan Pamuk would be unknown outside his native Turkey; thanks to translations, his haunting novel *Kar* can be found in Mexico City airport under the title *Nieve*, bought in Berlin bookshops as *Schnee* and ordered from Amazon.com in its English version, *Snow*. Translation paved the way for Pamuk to win the 2006 Nobel Prize in Literature, and it is in translation that he and a host of other writers will usually be read in world literature courses.

Yet translation has long had a bad reputation. How can any translation convey a novelist's nuances of meaning or a poet's delicate verbal music? *Traduttore traditore*, as an old adage goes, slyly illustrating its point by its own untranslatability – "Translators are betrayers" may convey the general sense, but the English paraphrase loses the pithy playfulness of the Italian original. This proverb is quoted near the start of a classic discussion of translation's limitations, a 1937 essay by the Spanish philosopher José Ortega y Gasset, "La Miseria y el esplendor de la traducción." Ortega y Gasset's title implicitly links translation to prostitution, as it echoes the title of Balzac's novel *Splendeurs et misères des courtisanes* – pointedly differing from Balzac by giving the misery pride of place over the splendor. At the same time, though, Ortega y Gasset makes creative use of Balzac's title precisely by translating it, and he presents his essay as an account of a conversation held in Paris, presumably originally in French but now rendered in sparkling Spanish. His theme, in fact, is that translation is as necessary as it is impossible – an emblem of the utopian striving of human culture at its best.

The problems of cultural and linguistic difference take many forms and often admit of various possible solutions. This chapter will discuss the potentials and pitfalls of translation, outlining issues we should be aware of as we read translated works. By attending to the choices a translator has made, we can better appreciate the results and read in awareness of the translator's biases. Read intelligently, an excellent translation can be seen as an expansive transformation of the original, a concrete manifestation of cultural exchange and a new stage in a work's life as it moves from its first home out into the world.

Imitation, Paraphrase, and Metaphrase

Translation is at once a linguistic and a cultural project. Every serious translator has to confront the particular challenges raised in both dimensions by the text to be translated: How close should the translation stay to the verbal form of the original? Should a poem's meter and rhyme scheme be reproduced, modified, or abandoned? Should an older classic be made to sound modern or archaic? If a character's name has a meaning in the original language, should it be translated or kept as is? The first translator of Voltaire's *Candide,* in 1759, called the book and its hero *Candid,* apparently fearing that English readers would be thrown off by the French "e" and miss the point of the name. If a name is kept as is, should a footnote explain the meaning? The elusive heroine of Orhan Pamuk's novel *The Black Book* is named Rüya, which means "dream" in Turkish. Not wanting to use a footnote, the translator added in an explanatory phrase, having the narrator speak of "Rüya, which was also the Turkish word for *dream*" (8), conveying the meaning at the cost of a slightly jarring insertion. If a language allows paragraph-long sentences that are not customary in English – as is the case for Pamuk's Turkish – should these be preserved in an English translation or broken up into more manageable units? More generally, should a translation read smoothly and fluently, hardly feeling like a translation at all, or should it preserve some unusual verbal flavor, respecting the original's foreignness?

Translations can be located along a spectrum running from strict literalism to free adaptation. As long ago as 1680, the poet John Dryden discussed this question in his preface to a translation of Ovid. He described the extreme of literalism as "metaphrase." By metaphrase he meant word-for-word translation, the mechanical substitution of the closest possible equivalent for each word or phrase in the original, together with the retention in poetry of the original meter and rhyme scheme. Dryden had little patience for metaphrase, describing it as a "servile" mode of translation. As he says,

> the Verbal Copyer is incumber'd with so many difficulties at once, that he can never disentangle himself from all. He is to consider at the same time the thought of the Authour, and his words, and to find out the Counterpart to each in another Language: and besides this he is to confine himself to the compass of Numbers, and the Slavery of Rhyme. 'Tis much like dancing on Ropes with fetter'd Leggs: A man may shun a fall by using Caution, but the gracefulness of Motion is not to be expected: and when we have said the best of it, 'tis but a foolish Task. . . . (Dryden 39)

Shaking off these fetters, translators of Dryden's day often resorted to making very free translations indeed. Dryden labels such translations "imitations," versions that use the original work as a starting point for a fresh creation in the new language. In such a case the translator attempts "to write, as he supposes, that Authour would have done, had he liv'd in our Age, and in our Country" (40). A well-done free translation can have an integrity of its own, and it may succeed with readers by fitting in with their literary taste. Alexander Pope, for example, created very popular translations of Homer that rendered the epics' unrhymed hexameters as elegant five-beat couplets, the form he and his English contemporaries preferred to use for narrative poetry.

Though such a free adaptation can help a foreign work reach readers abroad, Dryden doesn't think the result truly does justice to the original, since "he who is inquisitive to know an Authours thoughts will be disappointed in his expectation. And 'tis not always that a man will be contented to have a Present made him, when he expects the payment of a Debt" (40). Dryden's idea of indebtedness is not just literary but moral: the translator has a responsibility to the original text and should strive to convey its force and meaning. To achieve this, Dryden argues for the sort of translation he labels "paraphrase," a happy medium in between metaphrase and imitation – neither fettered to the original nor abandoning it, but striving for a workable balance of fidelity and freedom.

All three of Dryden's modes of translation can still be found today, and each has its uses. Computer programs can now produce adequate literal translations at least of instruction manuals, while word-for-word translations often accompany student editions of an original-language literary text, as an aid to reading for those who have a basic knowledge of the language. Free imitations can give new life to a text that is fragmentary or obscure, enabling it to reach a general readership that would be put off by pages bristling with footnotes, brackets, and ellipses. Dryden himself allows that the ancient Greek poet Pindar "is generally known to be a dark writer . . . and leave his Reader at a Gaze. So wild and ungovernable a Poet cannot be translated literally, his Genius is too strong to bear a Chain, and *Sampson* like he shakes it off" (40). Yet most literary translation today falls within the middle range that Dryden calls "paraphrase." Within the middle range of flexibly faithful translations, translators have many choices to make; the balance of this chapter will outline these choices and discuss ways we can approach them as readers.

Comparing Translations

If we take different translations of an author and set them side by side, it soon becomes apparent that the translators' choices are at once linguistic and social. We may not often have the time to read entire works in multiple translations, but comparing even brief passages can reveal a host of choices that different translators have made. Their literary and cultural values, and their sense of their readers' expectations, become clear as we begin to notice patterns of contrast from one translation to another. As examples we can look at passages from *Candide*. Voltaire's satirical masterpiece has often been translated over the past two and a half centuries, giving us a window into the evolution of translation over time as well as across the English Channel and the Atlantic Ocean.

Interestingly, Voltaire actually presented his book as a translation from the outset. Rather than publish his religiously and sexually scandalous tale under his own name, he had the title page declare that *Candide, ou l'optimisme* was "Traduit de l'Allemand de Mr. le Docteur RALPH" (translated from the German of Dr. Ralph). Published in 1759, *Candide* was an immediate success, and it was quickly translated into English, published in London within months under the title *Candid: or, All for the Best. By*

M. de Voltaire. Later that year, apparently responding to some suspicion that this English-language work was a forgery in Voltaire's name, a second edition was still more explicit:

C A N D I D :

OR,

All   for   the   Beſt.

Tranſlated from the French of

M. DE **VOLTAIRE.**

The SECOND EDITION, *carefully reviſed*

and corrected.

The fiction of translation thus became a reality, and with Voltaire prominently named as the author.

Voltaire could hardly have been pleased to be exposed in this way – his earlier writings had led to his imprisonment in the Bastille and a period of banishment from France – but authors of his day had no control over foreign publication of their works. The London publishers chose to capitalize on the market value of Voltaire's name, not caring what trouble he might get into at home as a result. Undaunted, however, when he brought out a revised version of his book in 1761, Voltaire took comic advantage of the liberty of translation, and expanded his subtitle by adding *Avec les additions qu'on a trouvées dans le poche du docteur, lorsqu'il mourût à Minden, l'an de grace 1759* (with the additions found in the doctor's pocket when he died at Minden in the Year of Our Lord 1759). In this way Voltaire suggests that his "translation" marks an improvement over the original: it is enhanced with unpublished material found in the fictional author's pocket at his death on a battlefield of the Seven Years' War, still raging as Voltaire wrote. In "The Task of the Translator," Walter Benjamin wrote that "a translation issues from the original – not so much from its life as from its afterlife" (Benjamin 71). Voltaire would agree: *Candide* took on new life after the death of "Mr. le Docteur RALPH."

Candide's unfolding afterlife can be seen in the following examples. In the first, Voltaire's heroine Cunégonde has been forced by circumstances to take two lovers at once, Portugal's Grand Inquisitor and a rich Jewish merchant, Issachar. The merchant has reluctantly accepted the arrangement with the Inquisitor but flies into a rage when Cunégonde's childhood sweetheart Candide appears on the scene:

> Cet Issachar était le plus colérique Hébreu qu'on eût vu dans Israël, depuis la captivité en Babylone. "Quoi! dit-il, chienne de galiléenne, ce n'est pas assez de monsieur l'inquisiteur? Il faut que ce coquin partage aussi avec moi?" (Voltaire, *Candide*; *Romans et contes*, 180)

The anonymous 1759 translation renders this diatribe as follows:

> This said Issachar was the most choleric Hebrew that had been ever seen in Israel since the captivity of Babylon. What! said he, thou b—h of a Galilean, was not the inquisitor enough for thee? Must this rascal also come in for a share with me? (Voltaire, *Candid*, 29)

In good eighteenth-century fashion, the translator accurately translates the insulting *chienne* as "bitch" but veils the vulgarism with a dash. Voltaire's overall style is well conveyed, reflecting common period usage on both sides of the English Channel. If we now turn to a Victorian-era translation, it appears to be merely a minimal updating of the 1759 translation – with one notable exception, for the bitch has lost her bite:

> This Issachar was the most choleric Hebrew that had been seen in Israel since the captivity in Babylon. "What," said he, "you dog of a Galilean, is it not enough to share with Monsieur the inquisitor? but must this varlet also share with me?" (Voltaire, *Complete Romances*, 133)

Issachar's insult comes through in full force in two recent translations, which restore the language of the 1759 version, without needing the fig leaf of the dash:

> This Issachar was the most choleric Hebrew seen in Israel since the Babylonian captivity.
> – What's this, says he, you bitch of a Christian, you're not satisfied with the Grand Inquisitor? Do I have to share you with this rascal, too? (Adams tr. [1991], 532)

This Issachar was the most hot-tempered Hebrew seen in Israel since the Babylonian captivity.

"What!" he said. "You Christian bitch, you are not satisfied with the Inquisitor? I have to share you with this scoundrel too?" (Gordon tr. [1998], 288)

Each translation shows its own approach here to Voltaire's lively language. Adams keeps a certain period flavor in his vocabulary ("choleric"), in his phrasing ("you bitch of a Christian"), and even in his punctuation (no quotation marks), while Gordon generally aims for a fast-paced, modern feel ("hot-tempered Hebrew," "you Christian bitch"). Both, however, choose to alter one period-bound term, Issachar's calling Cunégonde a "Galilean." Unlike the earlier translators, both Adams and Gordon render this as "Christian." What is behind this change?

In Voltaire's time, "Galilean" was regarded as a Jewish term of abuse for a follower of Jesus, intended as an insult in class terms, as certain New Testament passages suggest; according to a theological treatise from 1686 cited in the *Oxford English Dictionary*, "when the Jews called one a Galilean, they meant an inconsiderable person." Adams and Gordon have both realized that no one today would understand "Galilean" to be a synonym for "low-class Christian," and so they prefer to give the basic underlying meaning of Voltaire's term. Perhaps they might better have kept "Galilean" and inserted a footnote of explanation, or added in a clarifying phrase like "country bumpkin" or "white trash." Instead, they made a reasonable choice to keep things simple and move the dialogue swiftly along, most likely feeling that Issachar's attitudes are clear enough from the rest of his speech.

At first it may seem that a nuance has been lost in translation here, but in this case the crucial shift has occurred over time rather than across languages. Readers of Voltaire in French today will also miss the point of Issachar's insulting reference to Galileans. Original-language editions are expected to leave the author's wording intact, even though *galiléenne* is now essentially meaningless today; the greater freedom of translation gives current English readers a real advantage over French readers in understanding Voltaire's meaning.

If a comparison of versions can reveal significant patterns of difference among translations, the use of two or three translations can also aid us in getting a better sense of the original work. Even if we can't read the source language ourselves, we can use translations to triangulate our way toward a better sense of the original than any one version can give us on its own.

This can be seen if we look at another passage from our *Candide* translations without recourse to the French. In the early part of the book, Candide and Cunégonde are helped by an old woman, who tells her story in Chapter 11. In the words of the 1759 translation,

> I had not always sore eyes; neither did my nose always touch my chin; nor
> was I always a servant: I am the daughter of pope Urban X. and of the princess
> of Palestrina. To the age of fourteen, I was brought up in a palace. . . . Now
> I began to inspire the men with love. My neck was come to its right shape:
> and such a neck! white, erect, and exactly formed like that of the Venus of
> Medicis. . . . My waiting-women, in dressing and undressing me, used to fall
> into an extasy, whether they viewed me before or behind: and how glad would
> the gentlemen have been to perform that office for them! (*Candid* 34–5)

If we look only at this translation, we have little way to tell how accurately it renders Voltaire's text. It reads well overall, but we may wonder about the woman's emphasis on the growing shapeliness of her neck. Do necks really change shape at puberty? Is the Venus de' Medici really so famous for that feature?

Eighteenth-century translators usually worked at high speed and for low pay, with results that can be rather slapdash. A look at the Victorian version shows material that is missing from the very first line of the 1759 translation:

> My eyes have not always been bleared, and bordered with scarlet; my nose
> has not always touched my chin; nor have I always been a servant. I am the
> daughter of a king, and the Princess of Palestrina. I was brought up, till I
> was fourteen, in a palace. . . . I began to captivate every heart. My neck was
> formed – oh, what a neck! white, firm, and shaped like that of the Venus
> de Medici. . . . The maids who dressed and undressed me fell into an ecstasy
> when they viewed me, and all the men would gladly have been in their places.
> (*Complete Romances* 136)

"Bleared, and bordered with scarlet" is a fuller description than "sore," more in keeping with Voltaire's vivid style. Even without looking up the French original, we may rightly suspect that the 1759 translator casually condensed the description of the woman's eyes – or possibly his typesetter just missed a phrase. The Victorian translation is useful here, but it only increases the uncertainty about the woman's beautiful neck, which is now described as "firm," rather than "erect": "oh, what a neck! white, firm, and shaped like that of the Venus de Medici" (136). Since when are necks noted for being firm? This translator has seen a need to correct the 1759 version, but we don't yet seem to have reached a satisfactory result.

Our Victorian translator has also introduced a new uncertainty: the speaker's father has suddenly become a king instead of a pope. Here the principle that Voltaire is vividly concrete favors the older version's named pope over the vague new "king." The Victorians were typically circumspect in religious as well as sexual matters, and it wouldn't be surprising if the translator has shied away from giving us a licentious pontiff. This hunch can readily be confirmed by looking at the modern translations, both of which reunite the Princess of Palestrina with her lover, Pope Urban X. Keeping the name also allows us to see Voltaire's own negotiation of the pressures of censorship, for he removes his immoral pope a step from reality: there was no actual Pope Urban X.

The recent translations also solve the mystery of the oddly attractive neck. In Adams's version, "Already I was inspiring the young men to love; my breast was formed – and what a breast! white, firm, with the shape of the Venus de Medici" (Adams 535). Similarly, Gordon has "My bosom was forming, and what a bosom! White, firm, sculptured like the ancient statue of Venus" (Gordon 291). The recent translators have parted the veil of Victorian prudishness, but that isn't the whole story, as the perfectly frank 1759 translator had also opted for "neck." The original translator probably wasn't repressing anything: he simply made a mistake. An understandable error, as we can see if we do choose to go back to the French text, since the word that Voltaire uses is "gorge": "ma gorge se formait; et quelle gorge! blanche, ferme, taillée. . . ." The most common meaning of "gorge" is "neck," and the 1759 translator went with that meaning without pausing to reflect that "neck" doesn't really work in this context. Much better would be "breast" or "bosom," which are secondary meanings of the French term "gorge," and which would change distinctively as the young woman matures. Even without access to the French original, the context itself would lead us to favor "breast" or "bosom" over "neck," and rightly so – at least for a European novel. We might choose differently in a Japanese case; glimpses of a bare neck are charged erotic moments in works from the medieval *Tale of Genji* to modern novels by Junichiro Tanizaki and Yukio Mishima.

We live today in a great age of translation, and contemporary translations are usually much better than those of earlier eras. Yet older versions can often be helpful in correcting the errors or excesses of more recent

Figure 2   Venus de' Medici, marble, first century BCE. Uffizi Gallery, Florence.
© *Alinari/Art Resource, New York; reproduced with permission*

translators. In Gordon's otherwise excellent version of the passage just quoted, the woman's bosom is "sculptured like the ancient statue of Venus." Just what statue might that be? Adams gets more specific, identifying the statue as the Venus de' Medici: but is she or isn't she? A look at the earlier translations will indicate that Adams got it right.

From what we have already seen of Gordon's goals as a translator, we can deduce the reason behind his erasure of the Venus de' Medici from the text. In his striving to reach a contemporary reader, Gordon apparently decided that the statue would be too unfamiliar a work to mention by name – surely a mistake on his part, given the Venus de' Medici's fame as a centerpiece of the Uffizi Gallery in Florence. In Voltaire's time, it was widely reproduced in engravings and in Sèvres porcelain; copies in lead were popular garden ornaments. Even if modern readers don't know her, they can easily Google "Venus de Medici" and see the statue's erotic power for themselves (Figure 2) – an option not allowed by the un-Voltairean vagueness of Gordon's unspecified "ancient statue."

How Foreign Should a Translation Be?

As we have seen with *Candide*, substantial issues arise for translators even when a work comes from a neighboring country and the not too distant past. The challenges grow all the greater when a work is farther off in time and in culture. How should the translation reflect the foreignness of the original, and how far should it adapt to the host-country's literary norms? Too much foreignness can produce a text that will baffle or bore its new audience, while too much assimilation may lose the difference that made the work worth translating to begin with. These questions go beyond the issue of the accuracy of individual word choices. Translators have two fundamental decisions to make: first, they must decide for themselves what they believe to be the original work's nature: its tone, level and mode of address, and its relation to the world around it. Having come to an understanding – really, an interpretation – of the work's meaning and force in its original setting, they must then develop strategies to convey the work's qualities to a new audience, adjusting for the differences of language, time, place, and audience expectations.

A text of striking variability, both in the original and in translation, is the great medieval Arabic *Alf Layla wa-Layla*, known in English as *The*

Thousand and One Nights or more loosely as *The Arabian Nights*. First composed in the ninth century, it was based on a Persian collection called *Hazar Afsana* ("a thousand legends"). The Arabic text kept the Persian frame tale in which King Shahryar, finding his wife unfaithful, kills her and begins marrying a different woman each night, killing each new bride in the morning. Families start hiding their daughters, and finally the king's vizier despairs of finding a new victim; his daughter, called Shahrazad or Scheherazade in different versions, insists on being chosen next, pledging to save the kingdom's women or die in the attempt. On her wedding night, after she and Shahryar have consummated their marriage, Shahrazad begins telling the king and her sister Dunyazad an engrossing story, cleverly leaving it unfinished as dawn approaches. Dunyazad begs to hear the story's end and Shahryar spares Shahrazad until the next night, whereupon she folds her first story into a second, leaving that one unfinished in turn. The pattern continues until the thousand and first night, when the king finally admits the error of his murderous ways and marries Shahrazad, who by now has given birth to three children.

To judge from the surviving manuscripts (all written centuries after the collection was first composed), the Arabic text at first had nothing like an actual thousand and one nights. Yet storytellers soon began to add in all kinds of further stories, originating chiefly in Baghdad and Cairo but some coming from as far afield as India and China. Over time, the *Nights* became a massive collection that includes over six hundred tales in its fullest versions. Nor does it feature only prose narrative. Poetry was the major literary genre in medieval Arab culture, and early editors began introducing poems into the midst of the stories. Sometimes they folded in classical lyrics by canonical poets such as Abu Nuwas (who came to figure as the protagonist in a number of stories focused on his love of drink and young boys), and sometimes the editors apparently composed poems on their own. The result is a composite text, mixing poetry, straightforward prose, and an intermediate mode of rhymed prose.

Eventually *The Thousand and One Nights* came to the attention of Western travelers in the Middle East, and a pioneering translation was produced in French by Antoine Galland, published in twelve volumes between 1704 and 1717. This translation was tremendously successful, and became the basis for many more re-translations into other European languages. Continuing the practice of many copyists and editors over the centuries, Galland felt no hesitation in enriching the work with further stories he had heard from a Syrian storyteller. Aladdin and Ali Baba first appeared in print in

Galland's French retelling; their tales soon became a standard part of Arabic editions, which simply re-translated Galland's additions back into Arabic. In a real sense, Galland's twelve volumes are not so much a translation as a new stage in the ongoing evolution of the *Nights*.

The first English translations were all based on Galland; only in the nineteenth century did English translators attempt to deal directly with the Arabic text. From that time onward, the *Nights*' translators have had to begin by asking themselves which text to use: one or another of the very varied medieval manuscripts or one of the modern editions with many newly added stories. And what of the ten thousand lines of sometimes mediocre poetry scattered through the tales? Should they be translated at all, and if so, how should the unfamiliar verse forms be rendered? How much cultural information should be given to help European readers make sense of the tales? Should such information be quietly inserted into the text or should extensive footnotes be added? And what of the various vulgarisms and erotic episodes in the *Nights* – should they be translated directly, discreetly toned down, or eliminated altogether?

Already in the nineteenth century, translators took dramatically different approaches to these questions. In 1839 an Arabist named Edward William Lane published what became the standard Victorian translation. Using as his base text an Arabic version containing only two hundred tales, Lane left out nearly half of them, seeking to avoid anything "objectionable" or "approaching to licentiousness" (Burton tr. 1:xii). He kept in some of the poetry but translated it as prose, and he rendered the often musical prose of the Arabic original in rather flat English. Lane's workmanlike, bowdlerized version went through many editions over the years, reappearing in the twentieth century, for instance, as the translation chosen for the Harvard Classics.

The starkest possible contrast to Lane can be found in the flamboyant rendering by explorer-adventurer Sir Richard Francis Burton, privately printed in ten volumes published in 1885, with another six supplemental volumes thereafter. In a polemical foreword to his new version, Burton belittled Lane's "unreadable" prose, with its "sesquipedalian un-English words, and the stiff and stilted style of half a century ago when our prose was, perhaps, the worst in Europe" (Burton tr. 1:xii). Burton returned to the attack in a long concluding essay that takes up the bulk of his tenth volume, in which he denounced Lane's prose translations of the *Nights*' verses for "the bald literalism of the passages which he rendered in truly prosaic prose" (10:222). Even more absurd, to Burton, was Lane's prudery.

Burton set himself the goal "to show what 'The Thousand Nights and a Night' really is" (1:xii) – in all its poetic intensity, its Oriental splendor, and its frank sexuality.

The differences between the two approaches are readily seen in the opening frame tale, in which the kings Shahryar and Shazaman are outraged to find their wives taking lovers in their absence. When Shahzaman chances to see his brother's wife appear in a garden with a cohort of serving women and slaves, in Lane's modest version

> A door of the palace was opened, and there came forth from it twenty females and twenty male black slaves; and the King's wife, who was distinguished by extraordinary beauty and elegance, accompanied them to a fountain, where they all disrobed themselves, and sat down together. The king's wife then called out, O Mes'ud! and immediately a black slave came to her, and embraced her; she doing the like. So also did the other slaves and the women; and all of them continued revelling together until the close of day. (Lane tr.7)

Burton gives this scene very differently:

> So King Shah Zaman . . . abode thinking with saddest thought over his wife's betrayal and burning sighs issued from his tortured breast. And as he continued in this case lo! a postern of the palace, which was carefully kept private, swung open and out of it came twenty slave girls surrounding his brother's wife who was wondrous fair, a model of beauty and comeliness and symmetry and perfect loveliness and who paced with the grace of a gazelle which panteth for the cooling stream. Thereupon Shah Zaman drew back from the window, but he kept the bevy in sight espying them from a place whence he could not be espied. They walked under the very lattice and advanced a little way into the garden till they came to a jetting fountain amiddlemost a great basin of water; then they stripped off their clothes and behold, ten of them were women, concubines of the King, and the other ten were white slaves. Then they all paired off, each with each: but the Queen, who was left alone, presently cried out in a loud voice, "Here to me, O my lord Saeed!" and then sprang with a drop-leap from one of the trees a big slobbering blackamoor with rolling eyes which showed the whites, a truly hideous sight. He walked boldly up to her and threw his arms round her neck while she embraced him as warmly; then he bussed her and winding his legs round hers, as a button-loop clasps a button, he threw her and enjoyed her. On like wise did the other slaves with the girls till all had satisfied their passions, and they ceased not from kissing and clipping, coupling and carousing till day began to wane. (Burton tr. 1:6).

Burton gives us details that Lane has suppressed, and then some; he added in the slave's minstrel-like rolling eyes, and he seems to have come up with the button-loop metaphor on his own. In Dryden's terms, Burton's version is sometimes more of a free imitation than a careful paraphrase, but he was intent upon conveying for English readers the dramatic effect that he had experienced in Cairo when hearing stories performed by professional storytellers. In its strange intensity, Burton's *Book of the Thousand Nights and a Night* is not a strictly literary text at all, but an imaginative re-creation of an enthralling oral performance.

Burton fondly recalled the varied modes of delivery used by storytellers in the Middle East: "The Ráwi would declaim the recitative somewhat in conversational style; he would intone the Saj'a or prose-rhyme and he would chant to the twanging of the Rabáb, a one-stringed viol, the poetical parts" (10:145). Burton was particularly proud of his ability to re-create the *Nights'* rhymed prose: "this 'Saj'a,' or cadence of the cooing dove," he remarks in his foreword, "has in Arabic its special duties. It adds a sparkle to description and a point to proverb, epigram and dialogue" (1:xiv). In the garden scene quoted above, Burton's "they ceased not from kissing and clipping, coupling and carousing" is much more effective than Lane's colorless "all of them continued revelling." Or again, where Lane has a jinni snoring in his sleep, Burton's jinni "slept and snored and snarked like the roll of thunder" (1:11). Burton realized that he could only convey the quality of the rhymed prose by forcing the norms of English vocabulary and syntax, and in his foreword he emphasizes his commitment to conveying the foreignness of the original: "This rhymed prose may be 'un-English' and unpleasant, even irritating to the British ear; still I look upon it as a *sine qua non* for a complete reproduction of the original" (1:xiv).

Later translators of the *Nights* have loved to amuse themselves – and clear space for their rival versions – by quoting some of Burton's most flamboyant passages and denouncing his style as "artificial" and "tortured," as the recent translator Husain Haddawy puts it. "What Burton bequeathed to the nation," he sniffs – or snarks – "was no more than a literary Brighton Pavilion" (Haddawy xxv, referring to the kitschy, Oriental-style summer palace built by the future King George IV in the early nineteenth century). According to N. J. Dawood, "What Burton gained in accuracy he lost in style. His excessive weakness for the archaic, his habit of coining words and phrases, and the unnatural idiom he affected, detract from the literary quality of his translation without in any way enhancing its fidelity to the original. The notes are far more entertaining than the text" (Dawood 10).

Dawood and Haddawy protest too much. To be sure, Burton's voyeuristic Orientalism justifiably irritates these modern, Baghdad-born scholars, who have seen too many Westerners projecting their fantasy life onto the Middle East. Even Burton's footnotes are excessive: they tell us far more than we need to know, for example, about Egyptian sexual practices and the shapes of Bedouin women's breasts. Dawood's and Haddawy's careful and soberly annotated translations have understandably supplanted Burton and Lane as the most widely read English versions. And yet it can't be said that either has finally done fuller justice than Burton to the *Nights*. Despite a Burton-inspired frankness on sexual matters, in other respects the recent translators have ended up producing trim, almost prim texts. If Burton errs through overreaching, his modern successors too often fall short in their urge to rein the text in.

N. J. Dawood's translation, published by Penguin in 1954 and revised in 1973, casts the tales in a mode of novelistic realism. Describing the *Nights* in his introduction as "the most comprehensive and intimate record of medieval Islam," Dawood tends to minimize the tales' poetic and rhetorical flights of fancy. "For despite the fabulous and fantastic world they portray," he announces, "they are a faithful mirror of the life and manners of the age which engendered them. They are spontaneous products of untutored minds" (7). In keeping with this understanding, Dawood writes in clear and straightforward prose, very much in Lane's plain style. In Dawood's version, the queen and her serving-women never indulge in anything so flowery as "kissing and clipping, coupling and carousing"; we are merely told of them "revelling together" – actually the very phrase that Lane had used a century before.

Dawood's commitment to a vision of the tales as realistic products of untutored minds leads him to leave out the hundreds of poems that offer pauses for moral reflection and lyrical reverie. Most remarkably of all, rather than interrupt the flow of the individual stories, Dawood deletes the recurring mention of nightly lovemaking and storytelling, with Shahrazad falling silent at daybreak and the urgent request from Dunyazad to resume her tale the next night. Like the poetry, the elaboration of the opening frame tale reflects the ongoing literary shaping of the material, which is no longer (if it ever was) simply the naïve production of untutored storytellers. Fidelity to the pure form of the individual stories has thus led Dawood to neglect the fundamental drama of Shahrazad's narrative race against death.

In the introduction to his 1990 translation, Husain Haddawy criticizes Dawood for deleting the poetry and stresses its important contribution to the tales' effect. Haddawy does include poems, but he omits many found in Burton, for he bases his translation on an incomplete early set of manuscripts. If Galland and Burton got carried away by the pleasures of an ever-expanding tradition, Haddawy's goal is to perform a return to origins, based in the earliest possible text. He relies entirely on a Syrian branch of the textual tradition, preserved in a fourteenth-century manuscript and several later copies. He uses this set of texts exclusively, even though they only include thirty-five complete stories, breaking off abruptly part way into a thirty-sixth story. As a result, Haddawy leaves out many of the most famous tales, and he even – bizarrely – omits the conclusion of the frame tale, in which the king finally comes to his senses and agrees to marry Shahrazad and adopt their children.

In his introduction, even as he admits that his source is "stunted," Haddawy insists that this limitation is actually fortunate, and he goes out of his way to disparage the far fuller Egyptian manuscript tradition: "If the Syrian branch shows a fortunately stunted growth that helped preserve the original," he declares, "the Egyptian branch, on the contrary, shows a proliferation that produced an abundance of poisonous fruits that proved almost fatal to the original" (Haddawy xii). Little wonder that he has no patience for Burton: offered Burton's concoction of poisonous fruits, Haddawy pushes his plate away.

Five years later, responding to complaints that he had seriously truncated the *Nights*, Haddawy brought out a second volume that included the tales of Aladdin, Sindbad, and a few other "late" stories. Yet even in this volume he left off the closing of the frame tale, as well as any mention of Shahrazad's nightly lovemaking and storytelling, simply because his preferred manuscript didn't include them. "Throughout, the reader will miss Shahrazad," he says with lingering regret, "but then I miss her too" (*The Arabian Nights II*, xvii).

Dawood and Haddawy are as cautious in their verbal choices as in their overall strategies; neither tries to follow Burton in creating a mixed, foreign-inflected English. Dawood remarks in his preface that "I have sought to reconcile faithfulness to the spirit of the original with fidelity to modern English usage. I have sometimes felt obligated to alter the order of phrases and sentences where English prose logic differs from Arabic" (10). In practice, English prose logic wins out over poetic Arabic prose in Dawood's smooth, workmanlike version. Though Haddawy attends to differing levels of style in his translation, nonetheless he forthrightly admits that "I have avoided the rhymed prose of the original because it is too artificial and too jarring to the English ear" (xxvii).

In a 1935 essay on "The Translators of *The Thousand and One Nights*," Jorge Luis Borges praised the "creative infidelity" of Burton and his French contemporary J. C. Mardrus, preferring both to the "scandalous decorum" of Galland and Lane (*Selected Non-Fictions* 97, 105). Dawood and Haddawy are sexually as bold as Burton, but linguistically they are decorous indeed. Their versions are refreshingly clear, yet Burton's over-the-top translation conveys qualities that his successors deny us. In its exceptional variability, *The Thousand and One Nights* is better read in two or three versions than in any one alone. Like Shahrazad herself, we may fatally compromise our experience if we confine ourselves to a single story – or a single translation – as we make our way into this most hybrid of works.

How Do Spartans Speak?

Not all translations require us to choose between ordinary English and a warped or "foreignized" hybrid in Burton's mode. In trying to convey the distinctive feel of a different language, translators can take advantage of the fact that there are many more forms of English than "standard English" alone. This possibility often comes to the fore when the source text employs more than one kind of dialect, as can be seen in the case of Aristophanes' comedy *Lysistrata*. The play was first performed in 411 BCE, late in the long-running Peloponnesian War, as the league led by Sparta began to gain the upper hand over Athens and its allies. In *Lysistrata* the women of Athens and Sparta unite to deny sex to their husbands until the men agree to cease fighting; Aristophanes highlights the comic clash of dialects and genders alike as he dramatizes his antiwar message.

The Spartans were famously plain-spoken and brief in expressing themselves; the term "laconic" comes from Sparta's region, Laconia. The Athenians regarded their own speech as proper, refined Greek, whereas they thought of the Spartan dialect as the speech of crude country folk, and Aristophanes took comic advantage of this stereotype in his play. If Burton and Haddawy differ in their conception of the nature of the original source text, Aristophanes' translators differ in the ways they strive to reach their target audience. Some translators have simply rendered all the dialogue in standard English, anticipating readers who want to get the story with a minimum of fuss. More inventive translators, however, have often made use of differing flavors of English, with the choice of dialect geared toward the particular audience the translator has in mind.

The British poet Paul Roche renders the Spartan speeches in a form of Cockney dialect, which will register with British readers as the language of the urban lower classes. Thus, a Spartan herald drops one "h" after another in his speeches: "Where's this 'ere Athenian Senate or Parliament? I got news. . . . I'm a 'erald, mate . . . 'aven't got bleeding nuffin. Give over babblin' " (Roche tr. 464). By contrast, the American translator Douglass Parker makes the Spartans into Appalachian hillbillies. As he says in a note, he gives them "a somewhat debased American mountain dialect" (Parker tr. 115), so that Lysistrata's ally Lampito says things like "Shuckins, what fer you tweedlin' me up so? . . . Git on with the give-out. I'm hankerin' to hear" (22–3).

Other translators have gone beyond language to history, seeking contrasting dialects that can resonate with modern equivalents to the war between Athens and Sparta. In 1959, the translator Dudley Fitts decided that the best way to convey this meaning would be to present the Spartans as Southerners of the Civil War era. Fitts makes no pretense of conveying the true tones of Southern speech; his Spartans talk like characters out of *Gone with the Wind*, in a Hollywood-style caricature that is intended to mimic the Athenian stereotyping of Sparta. In his version – which inserts as many "h"'s as Roche had dropped – Lampito declares that "Ah imagine us Spahtans can arrange a peace" (Fitts tr. 15), while a herald says "Ah'm a certified herald from Sparta, and Ah've come to talk about an ahmistice" (52).

Fitts drives his analogy home by having one Spartan soldier refer directly to the American Civil War: "Colonel, we got dressed just in time. Ah sweah, if they'd seen us the way we were, there'd have been a new wah between the states" (57). In Greek, the soldier is not referring openly to war at all. Suffering from an unquellable erection as a result of the women's boycott, he is actually expressing a fear that someone might come along and cut off his penis. Yet Fitts's change here is less random than it might seem. In the original, the soldier is recalling a real-life incident of 415 BCE when statues of the god Hermes had their faces and genitals mutilated, and these acts of vandalism were taken as anti-war acts. Rather than attempt to convey this obscure topical reference in his translation, Fitts has taken the opportunity to insert his Civil War comparison instead.

Thirty years later, Jeffrey Henderson decided on a more contemporary linguistic and political analogy. His 1988 translation makes the Spartans into

Russians, so that the Peloponnesian War becomes an early precursor to the Cold War between America and the Soviet Union. Like Fitts, Henderson sees Aristophanes' Spartans as comic caricatures, and so he gives them a fractured Russo-American dialect: his Lampito declares that "I go to gym, I make my buttocks hard," and asks, "Please to tell us then agenda of the meeting" (Henderson tr. 26). Like Fitts, Henderson takes some liberties with the text in order to bring out his political analogy: a character who is simply a Boeotian ambassador (*présbeirá Boiôtía* in Greek) here becomes Lampito's "Distinguished comrade from collective farm of Thebes" (26).

By these varied means, each of Aristophanes' translators has tried to bring the play's conflicts home to a modern audience, creatively warping language and historical reference to find equivalents to the conflict between the ancient Greek city-states. *Lysistrata* has not been well served by strict or literalistic translations, which have the effect of flattening out Aristophanes' language and obscuring his outrageous sexual puns. A man called "Kinesias," for example, is named from the verb *kinein*, "to move" or "arouse"; Jeffrey Henderson nicely translates the name, freely but effectively, as "Rod." The best modern translators all allow themselves liberties of this kind.

In choosing among the available translations, a reader will want to pick the version that seems personally most effective. This may mean that an American reader will prefer a Southern-style Sparta and a British reader will prefer a Cockney Lampito, but the reverse might also be the case. A British reader may find it distracting to have Lampito sound like Eliza Doolittle, while a reader in the American South may be annoyed by a version of *Lysistrata* in which Rhett Butler always seems to be waiting in the wings. In that event, a dialect from across the Atlantic may serve more effectively to get the general point across without wholly transposing the play into the present era and its finally quite un-Greek conflicts. The fact that the Peloponnesian War can be represented by one translator as the American Civil War and by another as a global Cold War shows the limits of any one-to-one analogy; the Peloponnesian War played out in terms not fully captured by either comparison. *Lysistrata* can be enjoyed in any of these translations, but we should read them in awareness that we need in a sense to translate the translations in turn, taking into account the ways the translator has interpreted the original.

Looking through the refracting lens of translation, we can best see the world it bodies forth if we attend to the translators' strategies as they seek to mind – and mend – the gap between then and now, here and there, another language and our own. As we become aware of the inevitable trade-offs that all translators must make, we can also appreciate their creativity as they build upon their predecessors and make a work anew. John Dryden could not imagine any adequate way to translate the free-flowing form of Pindar's odes; the measured couplets favored in his day were ill-suited to Pindar's "wild and ungovernable" style. Today, however, although we are centuries farther from Pindar than was Dryden, the resources of contemporary free verse make it possible to solve Dryden's dilemma. A modern translation of the First Olympian Ode by Frank Nisetsch uses varied line lengths, a shifting rhythm rather than any strict meter, and extensive enjambment to wrap the lines together in a forward movement suggesting the restless intensity of Pindar's style. In this eloquent rendering, the ode's opening can serve as an emblem of the power of poetry to shine through in translation across every distance of time, space, and culture:

> Water is preeminent and gold, like a fire
> burning in the night, outshines
> all possessions that magnify men's pride.
> But if, my soul, you yearn
> to celebrate great games,
> look no further
> for another star
> shining through the deserted ether
> brighter than the sun, or for a contest
> mightier than Olympia—
> where the song
> has taken its coronal
> design of glory, plaited
> in the minds of poets
> as they come, calling on Zeus' name.
> (Pindar 82)

Chapter 5

Going Abroad

In the preceding chapters, our focus has been on the ways works enter the realm of world literature by circulating out into the world, finding readers in distant times, places, and languages, often far beyond the author's own expectation. Murasaki Shikibu wrote *The Tale of Genji* for private circulation among her circle of friends at the imperial court in Kyoto; at most she may have hoped that her tale would continue to be read after her death by some like-minded souls in the same milieu. Yet she could never have imagined that a thousand years later her masterwork would be receiving multiple translations into English, a language that didn't even exist in her day, becoming a staple of world literature courses in North America – a continent entirely unknown to her and her contemporaries.

Works can also enter world literature, however, by a very different process: by bringing the world directly into the text itself. This can occur in one sense when an author reaches out to foreign literary traditions even when the story has a purely local setting. *The Tale of Genji* rarely ventures outside Kyoto, and a great deal is made of a character's exhausting struggle over forest paths to visit a woman in the distant town of Uji, which in actual fact is only ten miles away from the capital. Yet Lady Murasaki was already participating in a broader literary world: she constantly alludes to Chinese poetry and compares events in her work to famous incidents in Chinese history, and in her opening chapter Genji's father settles his son's social standing after consulting with a visiting Korean diviner and a specialist in Indian astrology.

Writers can engage still more fully with the wider world by sending their characters abroad. For fully four thousand years, literary works have often depicted long journeys of adventure in mysterious regions, whether for material or spiritual gain. Gilgamesh ventures to the distant Cedar Forest to confront its guardian demon and acquire precious timber, and he later crosses deserts, mountains, and the Waters of Death to visit his ancestor Uta-napishtim, seeking the secret of immortality. Odysseus spends ten years wandering around the Mediterranean world, in a compelling mixture of mythic fantasy and regional reality: "Many cities of men he saw and learned their minds" (Homer, *Odyssey* 77), in between dramatic escapes from exotic creatures such as the seductive Sirens and the monstrous Cyclops. Many later heroes have followed in his wake, from Sindbad the Sailor to Joseph Conrad's globe-circling merchant seaman Charlie Marlow. Other works are set entirely in a foreign locale, presenting images of distant lands and even alternate universes.

Writers who set their works abroad engage in a process of cultural translation, representing foreign customs for the writer's home audience. Like the linguistic translations discussed in the preceding chapter, these cultural translations involve interpretive decisions, first by the writer and then by the reader. Will the foreign culture be presented – or read – as comically nonsensical, mysterious and fear-inducing, or an exciting world of new possibilities? Does the work emphasize cultural difference, universal truths, or the pleasant surprise of finding an unexpected home away from home? How does the foreign society relate to the writer's homeland or to our own – as a friendly neighbor, an imperial rival, a land ripe for conquest, a lost paradise, or a thinly disguised allegory for the home society itself? This chapter will explore the ways in which writers have explored the wider world, looking particularly at how the foreign can both mirror and oppose the world at home.

Strangers in a Strange Land

In many literary works, a distant foreign land is at once dangerous and alluring. It is a place where customs are radically different from those at home, a difference that can be both liberating and disorienting. Free of the constraints of family and the society of their birth, travelers can reinvent themselves in the new land – if they can survive the transition. A classic early example of this pattern is the biblical story of Joseph (Genesis 37–50). As the story begins, Joseph's father has been showing favoritism toward him, breeding murderous jealousy in his older brothers, a jealousy that reaches a boiling point when Joseph rashly boasts of dreams that symbolically show them bowing down to him. They get hold of him out in the countryside and are about to kill him when they observe a caravan approaching, carrying spices to sell down in Egypt. These foreign traders provide a kind of safety-valve for the family conflict: the brothers resolve their dispute by selling Joseph to the traders, who take him along and sell him to the Egyptian official Potiphar.

Egypt was everything Israel was not: a polytheistic land of myriad temples and magical transformations; an imperial power, unified for millennia, with long-established cultural traditions and with rigid social hierarchies. A young foreign slave would ordinarily have no prospect of success in this environment, but God causes everything Joseph does to prosper, and Potiphar finds him so useful that he puts him in charge of his household. This promotion brings Joseph into daily contact with Potiphar's wife, who becomes filled with passion for him and asks him to be her lover. He refuses out of piety to God and loyalty to his master, enraging Potiphar's wife, who calls her servants and claims that Joseph has tried to rape her. In making her accusation, she emphasizes Joseph's foreignness: "See," she tells her servants, "my husband has brought among us a Hebrew to mock us!" (Genesis 39:14). Joseph's fellow servants might really have more in common with him than with their haughty, upper-class mistress, but Potiphar's wife shrewdly invokes ethnic loyalty ("to mock *us*," *l'zahak banu*) to override any solidarity among servants. The Egyptian servants take her accusation at face value, as does her husband in turn.

In this episode, Joseph is not only thrust into a foreign land; he is caught up in a foreign story as well. A popular Egyptian story, known today as "The Tale of the Two Brothers," had previously developed the motif of a false accusation by a spurned wife, combining this plot line with the fraternal rivalry that precedes it in the Genesis account. The hero of the tale, Bata, is working as a servant and farmhand for his older brother, Anubis, when Anubis's wife asks him to become her lover: "Come, let us spend an hour lying together. It will be good for you," she entreats him, adding – as a kind of bonus offer – "and I will make fine clothes for you." Bata rejects her with scorn, whereupon she tells the story to her husband, but with the roles reversed: "He said to me: 'Come, let us spend an hour lying together; loosen your braids.' So he said to me. But I would not listen to him. . . . Now, if you let him live, I shall die!" (Lichtheim 2:205).

As similar as the basic motif is, the two stories develop it in very different ways. The Egyptian tale proceeds by a fairytale logic. A talking animal reveals the danger to Bata, who flees, his brother in hot pursuit. Bata prays to the god Pre-Harakhti, who causes a body of water to well up between the brothers. As Anubis fumes on the far side of the crocodile-infested lake, Bata explains the truth to his brother, concluding, "As to your coming to kill me wrongfully, you carried your spear on the testimony of a filthy whore!" (206). Justice seems about to triumph, but then the distraught Bata cuts off his own penis and departs to a magical locale, the Valley of the Pines. There he cuts out his heart and sets it atop a pine tree; he dies but is reborn in the form of a bull. Still vengefully pursued in his new embodiment by his brother's wife, Bata turns himself into a tree. His promiscuous sister-in-law becomes the mistress of Egypt's pharaoh, and she persuades her royal lover to cut down the tree to make furniture for her. The unstoppable Bata enters her mouth in the form of a splinter; nine months later she gives birth, unaware that her baby is not the Pharaoh's son but Bata himself. The Pharaoh adopts Bata, who becomes pharaoh in turn, at which point he reveals the whole story and punishes his sister-in-law-turned-surrogate-mother, presumably with death.

"The Tale of the Two Brothers" can be compared not only with the Joseph story but also with story of Moses that directly follows the Joseph story in the Bible. Like Bata, Moses is adopted into the Pharaoh's household, and when he later leads the enslaved Hebrews out of Egypt via the Red Sea, they too escape from their pursuers through God's miraculous manipulation of waters that the enemy cannot cross. Bata's flight involves a crucial detour into the mythical Valley of the Pines, an otherworldly space where he lives for several years and apparently acquires his magical powers of transformation. Moses leads the Israelites into the spiritually cleansing period of wandering in the Sinai wilderness; by the end of their forty years' sojourn, a subject race has been transformed into a nation. In this way, the physical metamorphoses of the Egyptian tale undergo a metamorphosis of their own into a narrative of spiritual development and renewal.

There is no way to be certain whether the biblical writers knew the Egyptian "Tale of the Two Brothers," though the similarities are striking. There was certainly a steady interchange over the centuries between Egypt and Palestine, which was periodically under Egypt's direct control, and the Egyptian setting of the Joseph and Moses stories adds to the logic of a use of Egyptian motifs, much as a hero who goes to Prague today will often have Kafkaesque experiences there. Whether or not there was a direct literary connection, a comparison of the works is illuminating, both for their similarities and for their differing attitudes toward the foreign.

89

For the ancient Egyptians, the foreigner was anyone but *us* – one of the many tribes of "miserable Asiatics" just waiting to be conquered to the north and east, or a dweller in the fertile lands to the south, source of a constant stream of elephant tusks, spices, precious metals, and dancing dwarves. Egyptian literature makes little effort to differentiate one foreign culture from another, and distant locales are more often presented as magical spaces like the Valley of the Pines than as real places the reader might visit. The biblical writers, on the other hand, belonged to a small population at the intersecting periphery of several empires, and their writings often feature conflicting or ambiguous cultural identities. When Moses flees Egypt after killing an overseer who was beating a Hebrew slave, he is not restored to his ancestral homeland, as might be expected after his militant defense of a fellow Hebrew. Instead, he finds himself in an in-between space, the land of Midian on the Arabian Peninsula, where the locals mistake him for an Egyptian. There he marries a Midianite woman, Zipporah, with whom he has a son. Moses gives the child a resonant name: Gershon, derived from the term *ger*, "stranger, resident alien." "For he said, 'I have been a stranger in a strange land'" (Exodus 2:22, King James Version). Even the Promised Land was a region of competing populations in antiquity as it still is today. Enlisting Moses to lead his people to settle in Israel, God describes it as "a land flowing with milk and honey," but he somewhat ominously adds that it is also "the place of the Canaanites, the Hittites, the Amorites, the Perizzites, the Hivites, and the Jebusites" (Exodus 3:8). From the Bible's Joseph to Kafka's Joseph K., characters in peripheral societies and minority cultures have regularly found themselves on foreign territory even when they are at home.

Brave New Worlds

Real-life travels have paved the way for many of literature's imaginative voyages. From the time of Herodotus onward, people have always loved to read travelers' accounts of their adventures abroad, and literary authors have regularly taken inspiration – and have sometimes lifted entire passages – from books of travel. Travel writers in turn have often embellished their first-hand observations with colorful stories they have heard at second hand or made up outright. Fact and fiction clearly intermingle, for instance, in one of the most famous of all travel narratives, Marco Polo's *Travels*.

Having traveled to Asia with his father and uncle in 1271, the merchant Marco Polo returned to his native Venice in 1295 with little material wealth – he was robbed shortly before arriving home – but with a trove of stories. Caught up in a conflict between Venice and Genoa, Polo was thrown into prison in Genoa, and there he met a romance writer named Rustichello. This successful writer knew good material when he heard it, and at his urging Polo began dictating his memoirs of his voyages and his years of service to the Mongol emperor of China, Kublai Khan.

Rustichello seems to have embellished Polo's stories at times, even to the point of inserting some episodes from romances of his own. But even apart from Rustichello's contributions, Polo's account is a remarkable mixture of firsthand observation, tall tales, and pure projection. Polo insists that on their first voyage to China, his father and uncle had already found Kublai Khan to be eager to convert from idolatry to Christianity. The Khan asks them to have the Pope send out missionaries who could "demonstrate plainly to idolaters and those of other persuasions that their religion is utterly mistaken and that all the idols which they keep in their houses and worship are things of the Devil – men able to show by clear reasoning that the Christian religion is better than theirs" (Polo 36). Here can already be seen a major theme of the later literature of imperial conquest: the most enlightened natives are eager for Europeans to come and teach them the ways of truth.

A close reading of Polo's narrative, however, can help us glimpse a likelier possibility. Polo later says that Kublai Khan celebrated the major Christian holidays by kissing a copy of the Bible and anointing it with incense – but Polo adds that "he does likewise on the principal feasts of the Saracens, Jews, and idolaters" (119). Ruling over a vast empire encompassing many faiths, Kublai Khan sought to give a measure of respect to all, much as he cemented alliances with multiple marriages. Though Polo wants to believe that Kublai "was most desirous to be converted" (120), he nonetheless records the Khan's direct rejection of an invitation to convert: "On what grounds do you desire me to become a Christian?" Kublai asks Polo's father. "You see that the Christians who live in these parts are so ignorant that they accomplish nothing and are powerless" (119).

Even as he projects his European values onto the peoples he meets, then, Polo is faithful enough to record evidence that goes against his cultural presuppositions. Polo claims that Kublai Khan himself came to rely on his reliability and insight, employing him as an agent or ambassador on various missions around his empire. Still, to a modern reader, Polo's report is an unstable mix of close observation and highly colored fantasy. We learn the cost of ducks and geese in the Chinese capital (a bargain at six for the value of a Venetian groat), but we also hear of Kashmiri sorcerers who cause flagons of wine to float through the air from a buffet table to the emperor's hand – though Marco does not go so far as to assert that he ever saw one of these performances personally.

If the Khan's floating flagons would seem strangely at home at Hogwarts, this is because J. K. Rowling is one of many writers who have mined Polo's *Travels* over the years. Samuel Taylor Coleridge had earlier made Polo's account the basis for his romantic fantasy of Xanadu, where Kubla Khan builds the stately pleasure-dome where one can feed on honey-dew and drink the milk of Paradise. "The milk of Paradise" is a transcendent image at the poem's end, perhaps a metaphor for the poetic imagination itself, but it originates in ethnographic fact: Marco Polo describes a ritual that the Khan would perform annually at Xanadu, scattering milk to the winds as an offering to the spirits guarding the land and its crops (109). Elsewhere Polo calls the capital Kin-sai a heavenly city – less for its spiritual benefits than for the beauty and elegance of its many courtesans, who are "highly proficient and accomplished in the use of endearments and caresses, with words suited and adapted to every sort of person, so that foreigners who have once enjoyed them remain utterly beside themselves and so captivated by their sweetness and charm that they can never forget them" (216).

A growing stream of foreigners began to follow in Polo's footsteps in the ensuing years, and travel to distant locales accelerated massively after Columbus undertook his epochal voyage off the edge of the map in 1492. Appropriately, it was Polo's *Travels* that inspired Columbus to set sail for the kingdom of "Zipangu" – Japan – which Polo had described as an island of fabulous wealth, where the palace floors were paved with gold (244). Following Columbus's glowing reports of the Caribbean islands that he insisted were the eastern fringe of Asia, major expeditions set out to explore and conquer the "New World." Almost immediately new worlds began to be discovered in literature as well. In 1516, Sir Thomas More claimed that a sailor with Amerigo Vespucci's recent voyages to Brazil had gone on to find the ideal island republic of *Utopia*. Milton's Satan voyages from Hell to the "boundless Continent" of Earth, where he hopes to increase his "Honor and Empire . . . / By conquering this new World" (*Paradise Lost* 4: 390–1).

The rapid expansion of European exploration and settlement involved discoveries in both directions. In an Aztec poem from around 1550, the poet describes a trip to Rome, evidently recalling a voyage twenty-five years earlier when Hernán Cortés sent a group of native nobles to meet Pope Clement VII. Like Polo before him, the Aztec poet has shaped his memories into a form compatible with familiar images and ways of thought. Whereas Polo's Kublai Khan often behaves a good deal like the Doge of Venice, the Aztec poet recalls the Pope as resembling a Mexica lord:

> The pope is on God's mat and seat and speaks for him.
> Who is this reclining on a golden chair? Look! It's the pope.
> He has his turquoise blowgun and he's shooting in the world.
> It seems it's true, he has his cross and golden staff,
> and these are shining in the world.
>
> (Bierhorst 335–7)

European as well as native writers soon began to give their works a double perspective. In Shakespeare's *Tempest*, when Miranda exclaims "O brave new world / That has such people in't!", she is expressing the astonishment of an inhabitant of a distant island on encountering a group of *Europeans* who have been shipwrecked on her shore. "'Tis new to thee," her exiled father Prospero curtly replies (*Tempest* 5.1.183–4). One person's "new" can be another person's "old" world, and their comparative merits may lie in the eye of the beholder.

Imperial Fictions

A world may be new to us, but is it also true? Even a purely factual account gives a highly selective interpretation of what the traveler has seen; conversely, fictions of travel often include a substantial amount of real-life detail. Like the linguistic translations discussed in the previous chapter, these narratives are best understood as negotiations between two cultures. The stakes in this negotiation become particularly high when the work concerns relations between an imperial power and its colonies, since in these circumstances fictional representations can powerfully shape public opinion, for good or for ill. These effects can derive from the writers' own

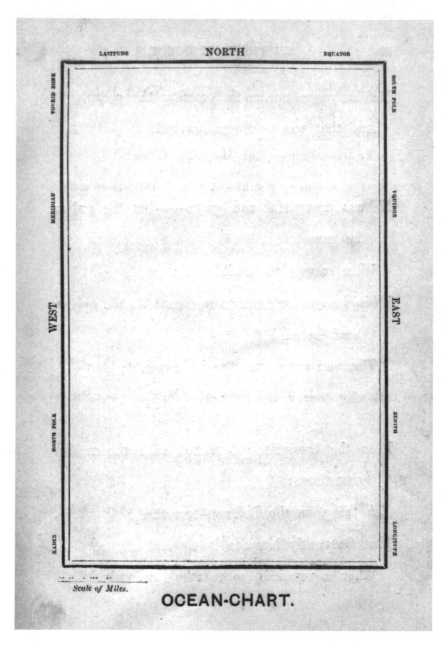

Figure 3 The Bellman's Map. From Lewis Carroll, *The Hunting of the Snark: An Agony, in Eight Fits* (London: Macmillan, 1876), 17

intentions or from later readers' reception. Marco Polo's thoughts were of free trade and unforced conversion; two centuries later, his admiring reader Christopher Columbus was dreaming of religious and political conquest. At the turn of the twentieth century, Conrad's *Heart of Darkness* helped spur the formation of a Parliamentary inquiry that led the British government to press for reforms in the Belgian King Leopold's practices in his private Congolese empire, and it influenced British readers' attitudes toward their own empire's goals and methods. Yet the violent and incomprehensible Africans who populate Conrad's tale look more problematic today than they once did.

A first question when encountering a travel narrative is to sort out its fundamental relation to reality. Some works are set in patently fictional locales such as ancient Atlantis or a colony on Mars, or they may carry clear internal indications of their impossibility. Lewis Carroll's surreal poem *The Hunting of the Snark*, for instance, concerns a quest for an imaginary beast that can be identified by five absurd characteristics: its "meager and hollow, but crisp" taste, its love of getting up late, its slowness in understanding jokes, its fondness for bathing-machines, and its ambition (Carroll 51–2). Carroll does provide a map for the quest, but it is just as disorienting as his description of the Snark. Faithfully depicting a stretch of open ocean, the map is framed with random notations such as "North Pole" (toward the south), "Equator" (at the top), and "Equinox" – not even a place but a time of year. Far from being distressed by this bizarre chart, though, the crew is delighted with it:

> "What's the good of Mercator's North Poles and Equators,
>   Tropics, Zones, and Meridian Lines?"
> So the Bellman would cry: and the crew would reply,
>   "They are merely conventional signs!"
>
> "Other maps are such shapes, with their islands and capes!
>   But we've got our brave Captain to thank"
> (So the crew would protest) "that he's brought *us* the best –
>   A perfect and absolute blank!"
>   (Carroll 47–8)

The Hunting of the Snark openly parodies the "conventional signs" of genuine explorer's narratives, but there are many less obvious possibilities, complicating any simple generic distinction between a novel and a guide-book. A literary travel narrative can be a poetic record of an actual voyage, or a semi-fictional account loosely based on the author's direct experience, or a fictionalization of other people's travel books, or it can be a pure fiction disguised as a real-life travelogue. *Gulliver's Travels* gives a prime example of this last option. Jonathan Swift sent Gulliver to impossible lands peopled by giant Brobdingnagians, minuscule Lilliputians, and talking horses, but he grounded his satire in down-to-earth prose replete with precise details: "We set sail from Bristol, May 4th, 1699. . . . By an Observation, we found ourselves in the Latitude of 30 Degrees 2 Minutes South" (Swift 4). A seemingly straightforward map helpfully locates the islands of Lilliput and Blefuscu off the coast of Sumatra. Some readers were actually taken in by Swift's deadpan style and travel-book apparatus, much to Swift's delight.

It did not take long for most readers to conclude that *Gulliver's Travels* is a bitter satire on European customs rather than a faithful description of exotic other lands. Debate continues to this day, however, about the New World adventures recorded by Swift's older contemporary Aphra Behn in *Oroonoko* (1688). Her novella – or "True History," as its subtitle claims – is set principally in the South American country of Surinam, which had been a British colony until the English ceded it to the Dutch in 1667 in exchange for New York. As a young woman Behn had sailed out to Surinam in 1663 with her father, who had been appointed lieutenant governor for the colony. Her father died en route, however, and after some months' stay Behn returned to England. There she found work as a spy before becoming a writer, chiefly of poetry and plays. Behn was the first Englishwoman to make a living as a professional writer, but as plays began to pay less well in the 1680s she turned her pen to fiction.

The question is whether *Oroonoko* is one of her fictions. Behn describes her story as having "enough of Reality to support it, and to render it diverting, without the Addition of Invention," and she asserts that "I was my self an Eye-Witness to a great part, of what you will find here set down" (Behn 8). These claims may be part of the fiction itself, but *Oroonoko* may truly be a memoir of Behn's acquaintance with the protagonists of her tale: the African prince Oroonoko and his wife Imoinda, treacherously enslaved in Africa and brought to Surinam, where Oroonoko led an abortive revolt culminating in his and Imoinda's deaths. Behn certainly insists that she is telling just what she saw personally or heard from reliable witnesses, and her story gains credibility from its depiction of local flora and fauna, such as the armadillo, "a thing which I can liken to nothing so well as a *Rhinoceros*; 'tis all in white Armor so joynted, that it moves as well in it, as if it had nothing on; this Beast is about the bigness of a Pig of Six Weeks old" (43). The reality – or the reality effect – of Behn's tale is even enhanced when she describes having used a real-life friend in an earlier fictional work: "We met on the River with Colonel *Martin*, a Man of great Gallantry, Wit, and Goodness, and whom I have celebrated in a Character of my New *Comedy*, by his own Name, in memory of so brave a Man" (57–8).

Oroonoko is an unforgettable polemic against the evils of slavery, and its impact is increased by the fact that Behn names real slave owners as she details the horrible mutilations that Oroonoko suffers before the slave-holders have him burned alive. Yet there are major elements in the story that seem much less credible, particularly a set of melodramatic scenes in Africa involving rape and incest, before Oroonoko and Imoinda are separately transported to Surinam where they are miraculously reunited. Scholars have extensively debated the question of how to take Behn's narrative (see Behn 199–265 and Heidi Hutner's collection *Rereading Aphra Behn*); perhaps *Oroonoko* can best be seen as a mixed form, a romance grafted onto a memoir.

Behn's own position in her first-person narrative is complex. Orphaned during the voyage out to Surinam, she is both a member of the govern-ing class and also a marginal figure, a woman with little power in a man's world; at several points she is shunted aside when the colonists are about to perform a new act of cruelty. Behn's marginal position has its advant-ages, however: she can serve as an objective narrator and as a mediator between worlds – both a member of the ruling race and also subtly iden-tified with her enslaved hero: "his Misfortune was, to fall in an obscure World, that afforded only a Female Pen to celebrate his Fame" (36). As critics have noted, Behn presents Oroonoko as an African version of herself: he is incapable of telling a lie, and always says what he thinks – including regularly questioning the morality of the supposedly pious Christian slaveholders. The narrative develops through Oroonoko's grow-ing realization that "there was no Faith in the White Men, or the Gods they Ador'd" (56). Readers can ponder just how far Oroonoko voices Behn's own views: her text may be a brief against Christianity as well as against slavery, or it may be a plea for Christians to live up to their true values and treat their slaves well.

As strongly as Behn opposes the worst slaveholders' cruelty, she endows her hero and heroine with remarkably European features, and represents Oroonoko as one of nature's gentlemen, less African than Roman in manner and heroic stoicism. He speaks in a Ciceronian style of somber eloquence, and even becomes known in Surinam as "Caesar." When his fellow rebels quickly surrender to the pursuing slaveholders, Behn has Oroonoko declare in disgust that most of the blacks are "by Nature *Slaves*, poor wretched Rogues, fit to be us'd as *Christians* Tools . . . and they wanted only but to be whipt into the knowledge of the *Christian Gods* to be the vilest of all creeping things" (56). Here Oroonoko anticipates Nietzsche's critique of Christianity as disguised slave morality, yet this critique has an ambiguous effect when an African prince levels it at his fellow slaves, especially when his speech employs imagery reminiscent of the Bible's description of Eden's satanic serpent. We are left to decide how far *Oroonoko* truly condemns slavery, and how far Behn leaves the larger institution intact, reserving most of her sympathy for the exceptional Oroonoko, with whom she can identify and whom she can assimilate to classical models.

Related questions arise as we read *Candide*, even though Voltaire makes no pretense of eyewitness realism. His rollicking tale freely intermingles real-life events (such as the earthquake that devastated Lisbon in 1755) with openly fantastic scenes, including a visit to the mythic Amazonian kingdom of El Dorado, where precious jewels are so common that children play with them in the dust. The satiric thrust of Voltaire's narrative is a frontal attack on Christianity and on Leibniz's pious philosophical theory that God has given humanity the best of all possible worlds. Europe offers many opportunities for Voltaire to illustrate the random violence of nature and the self-seeking hypocrisy of all religious people, but not content with illustrating his themes in scenes from Germany to Portugal to Constantinople, Voltaire sends Candide and Cunégonde to South America. This new venue gives Voltaire the chance to show the viciousness of European treatment of nonwhites, and to portray virtuous cannibals as models of an alien and yet higher morality.

As he sails toward South America, Candide experiences a resurgence of his sorely tried optimism. "All will be well," he declares; "the sea of this new world is already better than those of Europe, calmer and with steadier winds. Surely it is the New World which is the best of all possible worlds" (Voltaire, Adams tr. 534). No, it isn't: Candide and Cunégonde are robbed and abused just as readily in Argentina as at home. They have misadventures all around the continent, with the pointed exception of splendid treatment in the rationalist paradise of El Dorado. In a nod to *Oroonoko* – which had received its first French translation some years before – Voltaire even gives Candide a stopover in Surinam. There a native offers a Behn-style lesson in the realities of slave labor: "If we catch a finger in the sugar mill where we work, they cut off our hand; if we try to run away, they cut off our leg: I have undergone both these experiences. This is the price of the sugar you eat in Europe" (552).

The native inhabitants assist Voltaire in undercutting Christian values. When Candide and his mixed-race servant Cacambo escape from a vicious group of Jesuits by donning Jesuit disguise, they flee into the wilderness but are then caught by a band of cannibals, who start preparing to eat them. Candide protests that the cannibals are violating Christian ethics, but this argument gets him nowhere. Cacambo addresses their captors far more persuasively, arguing that they are common enemies of the Jesuits: "Gentlemen," said Cacambo, "you have a mind to eat a Jesuit today? An excellent idea; nothing is more proper than to treat one's enemies so. Indeed, the law of nature teaches us to kill our neighbor, and that's how men behave the whole world over. Though we Europeans don't exercise our right to eat our neighbors, the reason is simply that we find it easy to get a good meal elsewhere" (545). The cannibals rejoice at the discovery of these anti-Jesuit allies and instantly let their captives free.

Voltaire's often absurdist tale relies on caricature rather than three-dimensional portrayals, but some of his caricatures come rather too close for comfort to real-world racial stereotyping. When Candide and Cacambo first come upon the cannibal tribe in Paraguay, two naked native women are being pursued by monkeys snapping at their buttocks. Candide shoots the monkeys dead, but instead of thanking him, the Indian maidens weep bitterly over the loss of their simian lovers (544). If Voltaire's natives are an uneasy amalgam of philosopher and ape, every Jew in his book is a mean-spirited and lecherous villain. This unsavory pattern leads the editor of our edition to insert a cautionary footnote in the final chapter, warning the reader not to take Voltaire's depiction literally: "Voltaire's anti-Semitism, derived from various unhappy experiences with Jewish financiers, is not the most attractive part of his personality" (578n.)

This high-minded footnote protests both too much and too little. Too little, because it reduces Voltaire's distasteful stereotyping to a personal reaction against several actual Jews, who by implication may really have been grasping, mean-spirited villains. More to the point would have been to note that the eminently rational Voltaire is not entirely free of prejudicial thinking of his own. Yet the footnote also protests too much in singling out Voltaire's anti-Semitism, which should be understood as part and parcel of his anti-religious militancy in general. The choleric, lecherous money-lender Issachar, discussed in the last chapter, is sharing Cunégonde's body with the equally despicable Grand Inquisitor. Voltaire's world becomes a better place when Candide runs them both through with his sword. The underside of Voltaire's rationalist zeal is a current of intolerance, a take-no-prisoners attitude toward his enemies. Both his anti-Catholicism and his anti-Semitism should be taken with a pillar of salt.

Issues of realism and fantasy, critique and stereotyping, have continued to recur in more recent times. *Oroonoko* and *Candide* can be compared, for example, to the journey undertaken by Marlow in Joseph Conrad's *Heart of Darkness*. Like *Oroonoko*, this novella was inspired by an actual trip taken by the author, who traveled up the Congo River in 1890 to pilot a steamboat for the Belgian company that was exploiting the Congo's natural resources with the aid of virtual slave labor. Conrad's ambitions as a writer took on a new social and political urgency as a result of this trip, and gave him the germ of his novella. One of his assignments had been to transport a dying company agent, Georges Klein, who became the impetus for the novella's awe-inspiring, megalomaniacal Mr. Kurtz, the Company's prize ivory collector. Marlow ventures upriver to meet Kurtz, only to find him dying amid horrific scenes of brutality and the collapse of European ideals.

The novella's devastating deconstruction of the imperial enterprise is grounded in Conrad's personal observations, and its impact is shaped by the reader's awareness of the reality of King Leopold's brutal colonial practices. Yet readers have been sharply divided in their interpretations of what we find as we accompany Marlow upriver. Do we see Africa, or do we only see Marlow's hallucination of a dark night of the soul, projected outward? Do we see the essential corruption of European imperialism, or more ambivalently the failings of an imperialism gone wrong, or are we being shown a primitivism so unrestrained and unredeemable that Conrad reinforces the racist basis of imperialism even as he criticizes it? This last is the viewpoint advanced by the Nigerian novelist Chinua Achebe, whose novel *Things Fall Apart* can be read as Achebe's effort to give the other side of the imperial story. He set out his case against Conrad in a 1977 essay entitled "An Image of Africa: Racism in Conrad's *Heart of Darkness*." There he sharply criticizes Conrad for denying his African characters the power of comprehensible speech, or any independent action of their own. Conrad, he charges, presents nothing more than

> Africa as setting and backdrop which eliminates the African as a human factor. Africa as a metaphysical battlefield devoid of all recognizable humanity, which the wandering European enters at his peril. Of course, there is a

preposterous and perverse arrogance in thus reducing Africa to the role of props for the breakup of one petty European mind. But that is not even the point. The real question is the dehumanization of Africa and Africans which this age-long attitude has fostered and continues to foster in the world. And the question is whether a novel which celebrates this dehumanization, which depersonalizes a portion of the human race, can be called a great work of art. My answer is: No, it cannot. (Achebe 794)

As late as the mid-1970s when Achebe published his essay, Conrad's novella was widely read as the story of Kurtz and Marlow's psychic struggles. To the extent that the book was seen in political terms at all, it was celebrated as a denunciation of the European imperial project, and few European or American critics gave much thought to Conrad's representations of actual Africans. Achebe's lecture was an important corrective to this glossing over the text's treatment of the African people who provide so threatening a backdrop for the Europeans' adventures.

At the same time, Achebe's critique also reflects a realist novelist's impatience with Conrad's modernist ambiguities. Conrad forces us to experience Africa through Marlow's eyes, in a kind of literary Impressionism, yet Marlow is far from an authoritative observer in the mode of Aphra Behn. Conrad destabilizes Marlow's narrative authority at many points, deeply undercutting any simple endorsement of the racial stereotyping in which Marlow as well as Kurtz so often indulge. The story begins not in Africa but on a pleasure yacht, the *Nellie*, anchored on the Thames outside London. The story is presented by a shadowy narrator who retells Marlow's tale with an undercurrent of ironic disbelief. As dusk falls, Marlow is wrapped in growing obscurity even as he wrongly supposes of his listeners that "Of course in this you fellows see more than I could then" (Conrad 43). Mocking Kurtz and the other company employees for setting up ivory as an idol to worship, Marlow sets himself up, the unnamed narrator says, in "the pose of a Buddha preaching in European clothes and without a lotus-flower" (21). Conrad is doing something tricky with his hero, who thinks of himself as some kind of Humphrey Bogart figure but who is shown rather to have the illusion that he has lost all his illusions.

Aphra Behn had added authority to her narrative by evoking her position as a woman free from the distorting influences of the male-dominated system of colonial power. By contrast, Conrad undermines colonial masculinity from within. Throughout the novella he subtly satirizes Marlow's residual imperial machismo, beginning with Marlow's early embarrassment that he has had to ask a well-connected aunt to get him his Congo assign-ment: "I, Charlie Marlow, set the women to work – to get a job. Heavens!" (23). At the end, back in England after Kurtz's death, Marlow goes to see Kurtz's fiancée and offer his condolences. When she begs to know her beloved's last words, Marlow cannot bear to uphold his usual, Behn-style standard of truth-telling: rather than reveal Kurtz's true final words – "The horror! The horror!" – Marlow claims that Kurtz said her name at the end. Here Marlow no longer looks like a commanding figure of disillusioned knowledge: "I felt like a chill grip on my chest. 'Don't,' I said in a muffled voice" (94). No longer the voice of authority, Marlow sounds like the victim of a rape attempt. Having gotten what she wants from him, the fiancée gives a cry of triumph and dismisses him.

Marlow tries to see imperialism as redeemed either by "the Idea" behind it or, more modestly, by the concrete practicalities of manly work, but the novella progressively undercuts both rationales. Marlow meets increas-ingly deluded promoters of exploration and exploitation, such as a group calling itself the Eldorado Exploring Expedition, who don't even realize that they are looking on the wrong continent for Voltaire's diamond-strewn utopia. Everywhere Marlow goes, he encounters grim parodies of work, from the faltering construction of a railway line to the struggle to repair his damaged steamboat without rivets, to the skulls carefully planted on stakes around Kurtz's compound. Conrad exploits the racist stereotypes of Africa in the Europe of his day, not to counter them as later novelists like Achebe will do, but to turn them against the European side of the encounter, showing deep similarities between European self and supposed African Other.

Where Behn elevates Oroonoko by making him a latter-day Caesar, Conrad undercuts the imperial enterprise by making Roman Britain an early-day Africa: "And this also has been one of the dark places of the earth," Marlow says at the outset of the story (19). He evokes the grim experience of an imagined Roman legionary voyaging up the Thames, "going up this river with stores, or orders, or what you like. Sand-banks, marshes, forests, savages, – precious little to eat fit for a civilized man, nothing but Thames water to drink. . . . cold, fog, tempests, disease, exile, and death – death skulking in the air, in the water, in the bush. They must have been dying like flies here" (20). England is described as though it were "darkest Africa," and night is falling anew as Marlow tells his tale. Marlow's return from a foreign continent has revealed to him an inextricable mix of civilization and barbarism at the heart of the British Empire.

Looking Homeward

Since the close of the colonial era, writers have continued to retrace the paths of commerce and conquest. A striking reworking of Marco Polo's *Travels* is Italo Calvino's magical, unclassifiable *Invisible Cities* (1972), in which Marco Polo and Kublai Khan have a series of contemplative conversations in the khan's twilit garden. The Venetian tells of the cities he has visited around the empire, describing them under headings such as "Cities and Signs," "Cities and Eyes, "Thin Cities," and "Cities and the Dead." Many of these are flagrantly fantastical locales. One city is made entirely of pipes and plumbing fixtures, in which nymphs bathe in the mornings; another city is perched above an underground duplicate of itself, where the frozen dead mimic the living above them; a third city is supported by a great net strung between two cliffs: "Suspended over the abyss, the life of Octavia's inhabitants is less uncertain than in other cities. They know the net will last only so long" (75).

Each chapter is a gemlike prose poem describing an emblematic city, replete with imagery from Polo's travels and from *The Thousand and One Nights*. Women lead pumas on leashes down the street, artisan families specialize in making astrolabes or carving amethyst, and lucky travelers can be invited to revel in odalisques' baths. We seem to be immersed in an Orientalist fantasy of Burtonian proportions, but then oddly modern elements begin to crop up in this medieval landscape: dirigibles, radar antennae, skyscrapers. More and more modernity intrudes as the book progresses, and several of the later cities embody very contemporary problems. One city is so overpopulated that no one can move an inch; another city is about to be crushed beneath the towering mountains of garbage cast up around it; by the book's end, New York and Washington, DC (mentioned by name) have merged into a single "continuous city," as have Tokyo and Osaka. Calvino's text crosses the borders between past and present, East and West, utopia and dystopia, viewing the modern world through multiple lenses of worlds elsewhere. As Calvino later remarked, "The invisible cities [*città invisibili*] are a dream born in the heart of the unlivable cities [*città invivibili*] ... the continuous, uniform cities that keep on covering the globe" ("Presentazione" ix).

A true comparatist, Calvino's Marco never sees one city in isolation; all are linked in chains of signification and social meaning. He falls silent, though, when Kublai asks him if he has ever seen a city resembling the ancient Chinese capital of Kin-sai, notable for "the bridges arching over the canals, the princely palaces whose marble doorsteps were immersed in the water, the bustle of light craft zigzagging, driven by long oars, the boats unloading baskets of vegetables at the market squares, the balconies, platforms, domes, campaniles, island gardens glowing green in the lagoon's grayness" (85). As any Italian reader (and many a foreign tourist) would recognize, Kin-sai is a double of Venice.

Marco insists that he has never seen any such place, but Kublai presses him, asking why he never speaks of his native city. "Marco smiled. 'What else do you believe I have been talking to you about?'" (86). Calvino highlights the traveler's projection of the patterns established at home, and he extends Conrad's bold equation of the Congo River and the Thames. On the far side of the European imperial adventure, Xanadu and Kin-sai are no longer Coleridge's exotic otherworld where an Abyssinian maid will captivate the traveler with her dulcimer, just as Abyssinia (Ethiopia) is no longer a colony of fascist Italy. Instead, Kublai's empire becomes an image of a post-imperial Europe: "an endless, formless ruin" (5), typified in Venice's tilting campaniles and slowly sinking palaces.

Marco's beloved city is crumbling more swiftly in memory: "Memory's images, once they are fixed in words, are erased," he tells the Khan. "Perhaps I am afraid of losing Venice all at once, if I speak of it. Or perhaps, speaking of other cities, I have already lost it, little by little" (87). His loss, however, is Kublai's gain: "Only in Marco Polo's accounts was Kublai Khan able to discern, through the walls and towers destined to crumble, the tracery of a pattern so subtle it could escape the termites' gnawing" (5–6). Like Conrad's Marlow a century ago, and like Gilgamesh four millennia before, literary travelers continue to voyage along pathways set down by older migrants and earlier authors, making themselves at home abroad and returning to see their homeland with new eyes.

Chapter 6

Going Global

Over the centuries, writers have usually written for audiences at home, even if they sent their characters around the world. Jonathan Swift located Lilliput off the coast of Sumatra, but his satire was squarely aimed at the British Isles. Even a French or German readership was beyond his immediate concern, and he would no more have expected to be read by actual Indonesians than by Lilliputians or Houyhnhnms. Yet literary relations have long been incipiently global. Already in antiquity, writers and their works readily circulated around the Roman Empire's far-flung domains. Apuleius of Madauros grew up speaking a local North African language, Punic, but was sent as a boy to study in Greece. He wrote his *Metamorphoses* or *Golden Ass* in Latin, so as to entertain Roman readers with his asinine hero's adventures in Thessaly and Egypt. Comically apologizing at the outset for his unconventional Latin style, Apuleius compares himself to a circus rider who jumps from one galloping horse to another. He asserts that his linguistic metamorphosis mirrors his hero's physical transformation, and promises his readers delight if they will attend to "a Greekish tale" written "with the sharpness of a reed from the Nile" (Apuleius 3–5).

Looser cultural configurations have outlasted empires and have extended past the boundaries of any one region. The classical Arabic poet Abu Nuwas was read across a wide swath of Islamic cultures from Morocco and Egypt to Persia and North India. In the late nineteenth century, a century after the American colonies had achieved their independence from England, a brisk transatlantic trade gave Mark Twain a market in England and brought Oscar Wilde to America on a lecture tour. While still in his twenties, Rudyard Kipling – "the infant monster," as an envious Henry James called him – was being read on five continents.

The ongoing acceleration of economic and cultural globalization has brought the scope of world literature to a new level today. In the older imperial networks, literature usually flowed outward from the metropolitan center to the colonial periphery, with Dickens assigned as required reading in India as was Cervantes in Argentina. Colonial writers would rarely if ever see their works assigned in turn in London or Madrid, though older texts such as the *Mahabharata* and *The Thousand and One Nights* might be taken up abroad as representing the changeless societies of "the timeless East." Dramatic imbalances persist today in translation between more and less powerful countries, but literature now circulates in multiple directions, and writers even in very small countries can aspire to reach a global readership.

Paris, London, and New York remain key centers of publication, and as Pascale Casanova has argued in *The World Republic of Letters*, writers from peripheral regions typically need to be embraced by publishers and opinion makers in such centers if they are to reach an international audience. Yet many works find multiple publishers at the Frankfurt Book Fair, an annual event not tied to any former imperial capital, a venue where publishers and agents from around the world look for exciting new work wherever it can be found. In the late 1980s, several foreign publishers bought up translation rights for Milorad Pavić's *Dictionary of the Khazars* while it was still in manuscript, though this was a first novel by a little-known Serbian poet. Pavić's novel was published in 1988 not only in the original Serbo-Croatian but also in French, English, German, Italian, and Swedish. The next year it came out in Spanish, Portuguese, Catalan, Danish, Bulgarian, and Dutch, and within a few years it began to appear in non-European languages as well, including Hebrew, Turkish, Japanese, and Chinese. Pavić's international readership by now may exceed the entire adult population of his native Serbia.

Such successes represent a fundamentally new situation, affecting every aspect of literary production, from the outlook of writers to the selections publishers make and the choices available to readers. The new global literary market offers writers great opportunities, but it poses dangers as well. The meteoric rise of an internationally acclaimed writer like Salman Rushdie can set off a stampede of agents and publishers seeking more works in a similar vein. Milorad Pavić's sudden success was remarkable, but it wasn't exactly random. His *Dictionary of the Khazars* was aided by a confluence of two market forces: a vogue in the 1980s for Eastern European writing, plus the broad popularity of the "magical realism" associated with writers like Gabriel García Márquez. Rushdie had been the next García

Márquez, and now publishers were looking for the next Rushdie. If Pavić's book had come on the market a decade or two earlier, it would have been regarded as an eccentric work from an obscure country, lucky to get even one or two translations in small print runs.

The *Dictionary of the Khazars* benefited from the vagaries of the international market, but not every trend-fitting book proves to have any lasting interest. Second-rate knock-offs will be touted as masterpieces, while much better books can be ignored if they don't sound enough like last year's literary darling. Writers themselves may find it hard to resist going with the global flow, producing work that fits foreign stereotypes of what an "authentic" Indian or Czech novel should be. Alternatively, watered-down versions of trendy approaches can proliferate, written in a superficial international style divorced from any vital cultural grounding. As the novelist and cultural critic Tariq Ali has gloomily observed, "From New York to Beijing, via Moscow and Vladivostok, you can eat the same junk food, watch the same junk on television, and, increasingly, read the same junk novels. . . . Instead of 'socialist realism' we have 'market realism'" (Ali 140–4).

Real though these dangers are, they are surely no greater internationally than in national literatures. Publishers look to build on the latest successes in their home markets, whether these concern arctic explorers, plucky racehorses, or quirky Belgian detectives. J. J. R. Tolkien's *The Lord of the Rings* spawned an entire industry of fantasy books set in imaginary worlds, complete with maps showing the way to the obligatory wizard's retreat. British publishers today are trawling Edinburgh's cafés for the next J. K. Rowling, whose own Albus Dumbledore owes much to Tolkien's Gandalf the Grey. Whether they address a national or an international audience, the writers who prove to be of real importance are those who negotiate most creatively the tensions as well as the possibilities of their cultural situation. This chapter will explore a variety of strategies writers have developed for reaching audiences in a globalizing world.

The Glocal and the Delocalized

Writers in metropolitan centers do not necessarily need to adapt their methods in order to be accessible to readers beyond their home country, since many of their literary assumptions and cultural references will be understood abroad on the basis of readers' past familiarity with earlier classics in their tradition. Balzac and Victor Hugo have already introduced Paris for most new readers of Proust, who paves the way in turn for the Parisian scenes of Djuna Barnes and Georges Perec. Audiences around the world will have definite images of Manhattan and Los Angeles, thanks to the global reach of American film and television, however selective and stylized those images may be. Writers in Jakarta or São Paulo cannot assume any such general familiarity with their cities, and internationally inclined writers there and elsewhere have had to devise strategies to overcome the problem of cultural distance.

One method has been to write in a delocalized mode, free of any direct reference to the home country's customs, places, people, or events. A Renaissance writer could do this almost as a matter of course, adopting international norms of form and content. A Polish poet writing sonnets to his beloved Agneszka and a Dutch poet writing in praise of his Anneke could draw on a common set of Petrarchan rhyme schemes and metaphors. If they encountered their lovers' poems in French translation, even Anneke and Agneszka might have found it hard to guess which sonnet had been written for whom, particularly if both poets referred to them simply as "Cynthia."

The rise of novelistic realism in the nineteenth century led to a more pervasive emphasis on local detail and national concerns, making demands on readers to acquire a growing degree of local cultural literacy, an implicit barrier to reading new works from an unfamiliar region. In the twentieth century, however, a variety of writers broke with the norms of realism and began to set their stories in mysterious, emblematic locales. Franz Kafka's Castle and penal colony, Jorge Luis Borges's circular ruins, and the stark landscapes of Samuel Beckett's plays could really be set anywhere, or at least in any country peopled with arbitrary authorities (Kafka), melancholy linguists (Borges), and senior citizens in garbage cans (Beckett). Authors anywhere might choose this approach, but it is notable that the three writers just named were all born in peripheral cities (Prague, Buenos Aires, Dublin) traditionally overshadowed by the imperial powers that had long dominated their countries. All three chose to move beyond a provincialism they found stultifying.

To take the example of Borges, he began by writing realistic stories set in Buenos Aires, but he found this localism to be a dead end. In a 1951 essay on "The Argentine Writer and Tradition," Borges writes, "For many years, in books now fortunately forgotten, I tried to compose the flavor, the essence, of the outskirts of Buenos Aires; naturally I abounded in local words such as *cuchilleros, milonga, tapia,* and others, and in such a manner I wrote those forgettable and forgotten books" (*Selected Non-Fictions* 424). He came into his own as a writer when he realized that for Argentines, "our tradition is the whole of Western culture. . . . we must believe that the universe is our birthright" (426–7).

Far from feeling disadvantaged by his distance from metropolitan Europe, Borges asserted that Argentine writers benefit from this distance, gaining a special freedom and originality in using European forms and motifs. Interestingly, he supports this claim by comparing Argentines to European Jews, who "are prominent in Western culture because they act within that culture and at the same time do not feel bound to it by any special devotion." He argues that "Argentines, and South Americans in general, are in an analogous situation; we can take on all the European subjects, take them on without superstition and with an irreverence that can have, and already has had, fortunate consequences" (426). Imbued with this sovereign irreverence, Borges set his mature stories wherever it suited him, and collectively they span the globe.

A very different strategy can be described as "glocal." This term first became popular in the early 1990s among non-governmental groups seeking to "think globally, act locally." In literature, glocalism takes two primary forms: writers can treat local matters for a global audience – working outward from their particular location – or they can emphasize a movement from the outside world in, presenting their locality as a microcosm of global exchange. Some works display a movement in both directions, well expressed in *Omeros* when Derek Walcott's father assigns him his poetic life's work:

> Measure the days you have left. Do just that labour
> which marries your heart to your right hand: simplify
> your life to one emblem, a sail leaving harbour
>
> and a sail coming in.   (72)

To write for a global audience involves a conscious effort of cultural translation, and often entails direct linguistic translation as well. Unlike the early Borges, who expected his Argentine readers to beware of *cuchilleros* (troublemakers) while doing the tango to the syncopated beat of a *milonga*, Walcott writes largely for non-Caribbean readers who will not come to his poems with any knowledge of his island's environment, customs, or history. Walcott nevertheless embraces St. Lucia's history and the local features of its landscape, but does so in such a way as to teach his readers what they need to know to understand his lines. The opening pages of *Omeros* are dotted with italicized Creole terms for local trees (*laurier-cannelles, bois-campêche, bois-flot*), but these terms are unobtrusively explained or contextualized for non-Creole speakers, and the poem gradually teaches us a good deal about the island's history.

Walcott's linguistic and cultural self-translations build on a century's worth of experiments in glocalized writing, often refining techniques that were most influentially developed by Rudyard Kipling. Perhaps the first global writer in a modern sense, Kipling made a rapid transition from writing for a purely local audience to addressing a readership that spanned the globe. Born in India in 1865, as a child he became fluent in Hindi as well as English. He was sent when he was six to England for schooling, then returned to India at age sixteen. He soon found work as a newspaper reporter for the *Civil and Military Gazette* in Lahore. His first poems and stories – published to fill empty column space – were written for the Anglo-Indian community. They often leave place names and Hindi terms unexplained, and in general assume a good deal of local knowledge.

Yet Kipling was already writing as both an insider and an outsider. On his return to India in 1881 he had quickly recovered his fluency in Hindi, but he now saw his boyhood haunts with an "England-returned" perspective. As his works caught on abroad, it was only a further step for Kipling to translate his local knowledge for distant readers. He became adept at folding explanations and outright translations into his narrative, particularly after he left India for good in 1889, living first in London, then in Vermont, then finally settling in England again. His 1901 novel *Kim*, for instance, begins with a lively scene that sets the stage politically and linguistically for foreign readers:

> He sat, in defiance of municipal orders, astride the gun Zam-Zammah on her brick platform opposite the old Ajaib-Gher – the Wonder House, as the natives call the Lahore Museum. Who hold Zam-Zammah, that "fire-breathing dragon," hold the Punjab; for the great green-bronze piece is always first of the conqueror's loot.
>
> There was some justification for Kim, – he had kicked Lala Dinanath's boy off the trunnions, – since the English held the Punjab and Kim was English. (*Kim* 5)

Within a few pages, Kipling goes on to give a number of Hindi terms (*jadoo, faquirs, ghi, parhari*, and more), sometimes translating them in parentheses, sometimes defining them in a following paraphrase, sometimes shaping the context to suggest the meaning.

110

Kim is filled with colorful local details which Kim is constantly asking about or assessing for himself, very much to the reader's benefit. Thus when he encounters an old woman riding in "a gaily ornamented *ruth* or family bullock-cart," accompanied by eight servants, Kim observes them with almost the eye of a professional ethnographer:

> Kim looked over the retinue critically. Half of them were thin-legged, gray-bearded Ooryas from down country. The other half were duffle-clad, felt-hatted hillmen of the North; and that mixture told its own tale, even if he had not overheard the incessant sparring between the two divisions. The old lady was going south on a visit – probably to a rich relative, most probably a son-in-law, who had sent up an escort as a mark of respect. The hillmen would be of her own people – Kulu or Kangra folk. It was quite clear that she was not taking her daughter down to be wedded, or the curtains would have been laced home and the guard would have allowed no one near the car. A merry and a high-spirited dame, thought Kim, balancing the dung-cake in one hand. . . . (68)

Kipling multiplies opportunities to explain local customs to his readers. Kim is alternately a knowledgeable Indian-raised insider and an Anglo-Irish outsider. On the cusp of adolescence, he is both a child of his country and a neophyte in the adult world who needs to be taught the ins and outs of political intrigue. For much of the book he accompanies an aged Tibetan lama, who is adept at explaining ancient Oriental ideas but is also a foreigner in his own right, frequently clueless concerning Indian customs, which Kim can then explain. Still more clueless are many of the Europeans who appear in the story, not only Englishmen but also rival French and Russian agents, all jockeying for power in "the Great Game" to control the Indian subcontinent and surrounding lands.

The most interesting player of the game in Kipling's novel is Hurree Chunder Mookerjee, a "Babu" or Indian employee of the colonial British government. Kipling had used the name in "What Happened," a jokey early poem about the unwisdom of allowing trusted natives to put on airs and European weapons:

> Hurree Chunder Mookerjee, pride of Bow Bazaar,
> Owner of a native press, "Barrishter-at-Lar,"
> Waited on the Government with a claim to wear
> Sabres by the bucketful, rifles by the pair.
>
> (*Departmental Ditties* 8)

Hurree falls victim in a scuffle with less savory natives who have also been granted too ready access to European guns. A decade and a half later, the Hurree Babu of *Kim* is an altogether more complex character. If Kim is a virtual ethnographer of Indian society, Hurree actually makes ethnographic observations at every opportunity. He pursues this hobby with scientific zeal, his highest ambition being to become a Fellow of the British Royal Society. Given his colonial position, this dream is unrealizable, even absurd. Yet instead of mocking Hurree for his pretensions as he had done in his earlier poem, Kipling makes this unlikely dream a bond between him and the British Colonel Creighton, for "deep in his heart also lay the ambition to write 'F.R.S.' after his name. . . . So Creighton smiled, and thought the better of Hurree Babu, moved by the like desire" (175–6).

Hurree Babu's ethnographical skill aids him in his work as a government agent, giving him insight into the manners and motives of Indians and Europeans alike. He is particularly adept at disguising his own motives from Europeans by playing the role of the hapless, excitable Oriental. In a key episode, he gets the better of a pair of foreign agents who are completely taken in by his act:

> "Decidedly this fellow is an original," said the taller of the two foreigners. "He is like a nightmare of a Viennese courier."
>
> "He represents *in petto* India in transition – the monstrous hybridism of East and West," the Russian replied. "It is we who can deal with Orientals." (239)

Too often regarded simply as the poet of the "White Man's Burden," Kipling here stands firmly on the side of cultural hybridism, which appears monstrous only to the smug Russian agent who is falling victim to his own stereotypes.

*

Whereas Kipling wrote of the local for a global audience, other writers have chosen an opposite mode of glocalism: to bring the global home. Coming of age in Turkey in the 1960s, Orhan Pamuk found in this mode of glocalism a way to address modern Turkey's ambiguous situation in the world. Long the center of a great empire dominating much of the Middle East and Eastern Europe, by the later nineteenth century Turkey had lost its colonial possessions, and Turkish political leaders and intellectuals began to rethink Turkey's situation. In a process of Westernization that culminated under the leadership of Mustafa Kemal Atatürk in the 1920s, Turkey adopted Western-style military, governmental, and educational systems, even shifting its writing system from Arabic script to a modified Roman alphabet. Literary changes accompanied these cultural revolutions, among them the introduction of the Western novel as a newly prominent form. An increasing number of Turkish writers began writing novels, adapting European modes of modernism and of socialist realism to explore Turkish society and the nation's engagement with the wider world.

No Turkish writer has been more centrally concerned with the ambiguities of this engagement than Orhan Pamuk, a novelist who is thoroughly international in outlook and literary reference and yet resolutely local in his choice of material. Pamuk found in his native Istanbul – physically divided between a European half on one side of the Bosporus and an Asian half on the other – the perfect emblem for Turkey's double identity. In a series of novels and in his memoir *Istanbul*, he has probed what he describes as the Turkish desire to be someone else, often embodying this theme in characters who shift, merge, or lose identities.

In his 1990 novel *The Black Book*, a journalist named Celal has disappeared; he may have been murdered by someone angry at his writing – his essays ironically probe Istanbul's traditions and its troubled modernity – or he may have run off with the elusive Rüya, wife of his cousin Galip. Seeking clues to the disappearances, Galip pores over Celal's newspaper columns, one of which concerns a visit to a basement filled with uncanny mannequins. Their maker is a master craftsman named Bedi Usta, whose son shows the mannequins to Celal, remarking that "'the special thing that makes us what we are' was buried inside these strange and dusty creatures" (*The Black Book* 61). No ordinary mannequins, Bedi Usta's creations portray gangsters, seamstresses, scholars, beggars, and pregnant women, but what truly makes them stand out are their gestures. Bedi Usta had spent long hours in cafés memorizing all the small gestures of Istanbul's daily life, and he infused his characters with them: the mannequins are posed nodding, coughing, putting on their coats, or scratching their noses in precisely rendered Turkish ways.

Bedi Usta's trompe-l'oeil masterpieces gather dust in the basement workshop because no department store would have them: "For his mannequins did not look like the European models to which we were to aspire; they looked like us" (61). One window dresser admires Bedi Usta's mastery, but is firm in his refusal:

> the reason, he said, was that Turks no longer wanted to be Turks, they wanted to be something else altogether. This was why they'd gone along with the "dress revolution," shaved their beards, reformed their language and their alphabet. Another, less garrulous shopkeeper explained that his customers didn't buy dresses but dreams. What brought them into his store was the dream of becoming "the others" who'd worn that dress. (61)

Even at Harrods or Macy's, of course, window dressers might balk at displaying coughing beggars and depressed housewives weighed down with string bags; Western consumers too respond to dreams of elegance. What makes the mannequins truly uncanny to Celal is something much more specific: the people he knows no longer *use* the gestures preserved years earlier by Bedi Usta. In the intervening time, a flood of imported Western films so captivated Istanbul's residents that they abandoned their old gestures and adopted the ones shown on film. Now, "each and every thing they did was an imitation," as a nation of moviegoers practiced "all the new laughs our people had first seen on celluloid, not to mention the way they opened windows, kicked doors, held tea glasses, and put on their coats" (63–4). Shocked by this realization, Celal comes to see the dusty mannequins as "deities mourning their lost innocence . . . ascetics in torment, longing but failing to be someone else, hapless lovers who'd never made love, never shared a bed, who'd ended up killing each other instead" (64).

Pamuk expands on the theme of Turkish identity in an essay entitled "What Is Europe?": "For people like me, who live uncertainly on the edge of Europe with only our books to keep us company, Europe has figured always as a dream, a vision of what is to come; an apparition at times desired and at times feared; a goal to achieve or a danger. A future – but never a memory" (*Other Colors* 190). Pamuk's books explore the challenges to identity and cultural memory brought about by Westernization, most eloquently in *My Name Is Red* (1998). Set in the 1590s, this novel centers on struggles between miniaturists loyal to the stylized traditions of Persian art and those who seek to adopt a Western mode of perspective-based realism. Constantinople is tensely balanced – like Calvino's city suspended from a web – between Asia and Europe. People sit on carpets from India, drinking tea in Chinese cups imported via Portugal, poised between a Middle Eastern past and a Western future.

In this swirling matrix of competing cultures, Italian-style painting is starting to supplant the great traditions of Islamic art, as people are captivated by the idea that portraits can convey their individuality (a new, Western-style value) instead of more general qualities of character and status. Traditionalists object – one local storyteller has a painted tree declare its satisfaction that it has escaped being shown in the new realistic style: "I thank Allah that I, the humble tree before you, have not been drawn with such intent. And not because I fear that if I'd been thus depicted all the dogs in Istanbul would assume I was a real tree and piss on me: I don't want to be a tree, I want to be its meaning" (*My Name Is Red* 51).

History is on the side of the Westernizing realists, and yet they will never succeed if they simply try to be more Italian than the Italian painters they admire. *My Name Is Red* involves a search for a murderer among the Sultan's miniaturists, who proves to be a Westernizer who kills rivals opposed to the new style. Yet at the book's end, he realizes that his secret masterpiece – an Italian-style self-portrait of himself as the Sultan – is a failure, a clumsy imitation of a poorly grasped technique. "I feel like the Devil," he confesses, "not because I've murdered two men, but because my portrait has been made in this fashion. I suspect that I did away with them so that I could make this picture. But now the isolation I feel terrifies me. Imitating the Frankish masters without having attained their expertise makes a miniaturist even more of a slave" (399).

Like the mannequins of *The Black Book*, the would-be Westerner has ended up an outcast, torn between two worlds he can never fully join. Yet *My Name Is Red* is an exuberant book, filled with high and low comedy amid the aching loneliness of unfilled romantic and cultural desires. Pamuk's novel is, in fact, the best answer to the problem it so trenchantly poses: it is a vibrant hybrid that re-creates a vanished Ottoman past using all the techniques of the Western novel. Pamuk uses them and also transforms them in new ways; his book is divided into fifty-nine short chapters, each titled to announce its speaker: "I am Black," "I am Shekure," "I am a Tree," "I will be called a murderer." These miniature self-portraits link together to form a sweeping historical novel.

Like Borges, Pamuk approaches Western culture and his own nation alike with a sovereign freedom. An essay on "Mario Vargas Llosa and Third World Literature" reads like a portrait of Pamuk himself: "If there is anything that distinguishes Third World literature, it is . . . the writer's awareness that his work is somehow remote from the centers where the history of his art – the art of the novel – is described, and he reflects this distance in his work." Yet far from being a disadvantage for the writer, this sense of being an outsider frees him from anxiety about originality. He need not enter into obsessive contest with fathers or forerunners to find his own voice. For he is exploring new terrain, touching on subjects that have never been discussed in his culture, and often addressing distant and emergent readerships, never seen before in his country – this gives his writing its own sort of originality, its authenticity. (*Other Colors* 168–9)

Pamuk's emphasis here is on the local use to which the writer can put the techniques he imports from outside, opening new paths not forged by the national writers before him. In this way, a localized globalism informs the shape of the work as well as the themes within it.

In the process, Pamuk transcends the either/or choices perceived by the Westernizing murderer and the traditionalist tree. He lives at once in the Ottoman past and in the postmodern present, just as he lives both within Istanbul and beyond it, within and outside the pages of his fiction. In a direct expression of this doubled identity, Pamuk includes in the novel a young boy named Orhan, son of the book's heroine, Shekure, which is also the name of Pamuk's mother. In the novel's closing lines, Shekure bequeaths her story to her son, hoping that he will make it into an illustrated tale, but she warns us not to take the result too literally: "For the sake of a delightful and convincing story, there isn't a lie Orhan wouldn't deign to tell" (413).

The Binational and the Multinational

The global is often contrasted to the local, paralleling the dichotomy of life at home and life abroad. A major effect of contemporary globalization, however, has been to complicate the very idea of "home." Increasingly, migrant individuals and groups maintain active ties in two widely separated communities, keeping in close touch via cell phones, the internet, and jet travel. There are still writers who emigrate permanently, as did James Joyce, Marguerite Yourcenar, and Vladimir Nabokov before them, making a permanent home far from their homeland. Yet a growing number of writers divide their time between two or more locations, actively participating in widely separated communities and often writing for and about both of them.

For many years, Derek Walcott has maintained residences both in the United States and in the Caribbean, and by now should probably be considered an African-American as well as Caribbean writer. In key scenes of *Omeros* set in Massachusetts and on St. Lucia, the poet finds himself both at home and out of place in his birthplace and in his new country alike – a common theme in what can be called binational world literature. On his regular visits to St. Lucia he often feels like a tourist, his native island looking "like the print / of a postcard" (Walcott 69). Even as the ghost of his father gives him his life's mission to write about his island's people and history, an ocean liner looms ahead of them in the harbor. The cruise ship not only brings wealthy strangers who see the local residents simply as servants or as local color; it is also a troubling image of the poet's own escape into international fame and fortune, "its hull bright as paper, preening with privilege. / . . . Fame is that white liner / at the end of your street" (72). Living much of the year in Boston, the poet is ambiguously absorbed into the local scene there: leaving the Museum of Fine Arts at dusk, he cannot get a cab, as the cabbies take him for an inner-city African-American and refuse to stop for him (184).

Though this binational life is a constant source of uncertainly and unease for Walcott (or the character of that name in *Omeros*), it is ultimately a source of poetic strength, as he gains a breadth of experience and vision that his father never had. Though Warwick Walcott was a talented amateur painter and poet, his provincial life in colonial St. Lucia cut him off from the wider world, and his literary experience was largely confined to the old set of *The World's Great Classics* in the local barbershop (71). Living half the year in Boston, by contrast, his son can develop his poetic vocation far more fully, and when visiting Ireland he even has the ghost of James Joyce for his tour guide (201). Warwick Walcott himself makes this point later in the poem: appearing unexpectedly to his son on a Massachusetts beach, Warwick declines his son's offer that "We could go to a warmer place" (187). He can return home in due course, Warwick replies; but first, "you must enter cities / that open like *The World's Classics* . . . / Once you have seen everything and gone everywhere, / cherish our island for its green simplicities" (187).

A binational perspective is expressed in the very structure of Julio Cortázar's pathbreaking novel *Rayuela* (*Hopscotch*, 1963). First is a section entitled "Del lado de allá" (From the other side), set in Paris, where Cortázar lived for many years; this is followed by the second section, "Del lado de acá" (From this side), set in Buenos Aires, where Cortázar grew up. A final section is entitled "De otros lados" (From other sides), a set of "expendable chapters" of uncertain status in the narrative. This divided structure is crisscrossed by a second, alternative structure. While the book's 155 untitled, numbered chapters can be read sequentially, a prefatory note also invites the reader to skip around in the text, reading in a very different order outlined at the start, one that reveals the progress of Cortázar's migratory characters in a different way.

Three decades later, Salman Rushdie adopted an equally binational structure for his story collection *East, West* (1994). The volume is also divided into three sections: three stories under the heading "East" are set in India; three stories under the heading "West" are set in Europe; and three stories under the heading "East, West" involve movements back and forth between continents. The central story of this final section, for example, "Chekov and Zulu," implies dual nationality in its very title. Yet the story does not treat of Russians and South Africans at all. Rather, the title characters are two Indian employees of the British secret service – modern versions of Kipling's Hurree Babu – who like to imagine themselves as enacting roles from *Star Trek*, though they have modified the name of the Japanese Mr. Sulu: "Zulu is a better name for . . . a suspected savage. For a putative traitor," as Chekov remarks (Rushdie 153). He and Zulu regularly translate their experiences into *Star Trek* terms. When Zulu gets into a tight spot with a group of Sikh separatists he has infiltrated, he sends Chekov an urgent message: "*Beam me up*" (166).

Prior to this point, Zulu had disappeared during undercover work in Birmingham. As the story opens, India House has sent Chekov to Zulu's house in suburban London to make an inquiry. Chekov's conversation with "Mrs. Zulu" is a comic masterpiece of Indian–English dialogue, but it also reveals a suspicion that her husband has been involved in some shady dealings with his fellow Sikhs:

> "Fixed the place up damn fine, Mrs Zulu, wah-wah. Tasteful decor, in spades, I must say. So much cut-glass! That bounder Zulu must be getting too much pay, more than yours truly, clever dog."
>
> "No, how is possible? Acting Dipty's tankha must be far in excess of Security Chief."
>
> "No suspicion intended, ji. Only to say what a bargain-hunter you must be."
>
> "Some problem but there is, na?" (149)

The free intermixture of English and Hindi syntax and vocabulary – no longer italicized or translated as Kipling would have done – plunges the reader into the characters' bicultural life. As the conversation unfolds, we learn that the two men had adopted their nicknames as schoolboys in India, closely identifying with the multinational *Star Trek* crew as inter-global explorers: "Intrepid diplonauts. Our umpteen-year mission to explore new worlds and new civilizations. . . . Not the leaders, as you'll appreciate, but the ultimate professional servants" (151). In their adult lives, the two shuttle back and forth between England and India, engaged in political work and espionage. By the story's end, Chekov has been fatally caught up in repressive complicity between the British and Indian governments, while Zulu – outraged at the Indian government's use of terror threats as an excuse to oppress Sikhs – has resigned from governmental service, settling in Bombay as head of a pair of private security companies. These he calls Zulu Shield and Zulu Spear, now directly honoring the Zulus who had resisted the expansion of Dutch settlement in South Africa in the late eighteenth century. Thus futuristic fantasy and imperial history – *Star Trek* and the Boer Trekkers – come together in Mr. Zulu's bicultural Bombay.

*

Binational fictions often reach outward toward a multinational scope. In "Chekov and Zulu," American science fiction helps characters come to terms with their Indian/English world; in Walcott's *Omeros*, experiences on St. Lucia and in the United States are mediated by memories and dreams of Africa and England. Other writers construct fully multinational works. The action may cross many borders, or a single locale can be imbued with a multitude of ethnicities or else be inundated with the consumer products marketed worldwide by multinational corporations. Older national and imperial rivalries reverberate in these new global relations; understanding their dynamics can help us orient ourselves in the often disorienting worlds of global fiction.

The formerly military and now economic rivalry of Japan and the United States shadows Ryu Murakami's 1997 novel *In the Miso Soup*, whose lead character is an interpreter and guide for an international clientele of sex tourists, mostly Americans. In contrast to Orhan Pamuk's Istanbul, Murakami's Tokyo is a city whose inhabitants have no desire at all to become someone else; indeed, "Japan is fundamentally uninterested in foreigners" (10). The narrator, Kenji, notes that this isolationism may be regrettable, but it provides the basis for his living: the thriving Japanese sex industry is geared toward local consumption, and foreigners who don't speak Japanese need help in finding their way around. Kenji provides this service, for a hefty fee.

Though the Japanese may pay little attention to foreigners, Japan is awash in global consumerism, in both the production and the consumption of goods. America is a predominant focus of emulation and exchange; the Japanese media report every game the Japanese baseball star Hideo Nomo plays for the Los Angeles Dodgers, and even provide up-to-the-minute reporting on Michael Jordan's recreational golf outings (Murakami 13). In the novel, Japanese consumers think of America as the shopping mall of their dreams, as a prostitute tells a visiting American who compliments her on her English:

> "No! I want to speak better, but difficult. I want to get money and go America."
> "Oh really? You want to go to school there?"
> "No school! I am stupid! No, I want to go Niketown. . . . One big building, many Nike shops! . . . My friend said to me. She go to shopping Niketown and buy five, *ano* . . . ten shoes! Oh! It's my dream, go to shopping Niketown!" (20)

The pervasive presence of American culture is announced as early as the title of the novel, which is given in Japanese phonetic script in the original; transliterated, it reads *In za miso supu* – a colloquial Japanese rendering of an English expression ("in the soup") which has already been given a Japanese inflection in the naming of the soup as miso. Tokyo abounds with American and French names, plastered on stores regardless of the names' original meaning or context. The only person in the novel who finds this odd is Kenji's American client, Frank, who is puzzled that a department store is named "Times Square." He protests, "But Times Square is Times Square because the old Times Tower was there. The *New York Times* doesn't have a building in Shinjuku, does it? . . . Japan may have lost the war, but that was a long time ago now. Why keep imitating America?" (28). Kenji is baffled by this question and changes the subject.

In contrast to Orhan Pamuk's theme of Turkish ambivalence toward a culturally and politically dominant West, Ryu Murakami sees Japan and the United States as parallel societies. Japanese consumers may be trying fruitlessly to imitate Hollywood stars, as Pamuk's Turks do, but so do the Americans themselves. Arranging to meet Kenji for the first time, Frank says that he can be recognized by his close resemblance to the actor Ed Harris, but when they meet up at a hotel bar, Kenji finds that Frank doesn't look like Ed Harris at all – "he looked more like a stockbroker or something. . . . I just mean he struck me as sort of drab and nondescript" (6).

Murakami's multinational world is a culturally and emotionally flattened space in which Japan and America, former imperial rivals, have come to resemble one another. The apolitical Kenji learns this lesson from Frank, who recounts an analysis that a Lebanese journalist had told to a Peruvian streetwalker, who told him in turn – an aptly transnational circulation of information. The gist is that "the Japanese had never experienced having their land taken over by another ethnic group or being slaughtered or driven out as refugees," whereas "a history of being invaded and assimilated is the one thing most countries in Europe and the New World have in common, so it's like a basis for international understanding. . . . According to the Lebanese man, Japan's just about the only country in the world that's been untouched, except for the U.S." (171). Their once separate histories converging, Japan and the United States have become prime players in the new Great Game of the multinational corporations, turning people into consumers with comparable results of isolation, loneliness, and lurking madness. Frank is the book's prime case in point: he pretends to be a businessman who imports Toyota radiators to the United States from Southeast Asia, but he is in fact a murderous drifter who preys on prostitutes, modeling his actions partly on the movie *The Silence of the Lambs*.

Over the course of the novel – an edgy mixture of noir thriller and social satire – Murakami prods his Japanese readers to rethink their place in a global world. Frank appears at first to be a particularly ugly American, but as the story unfolds he comes to represent the bleak truth about a dehumanized modernity at large: "with all this social surveillance and manipulation going on," Frank remarks near the book's end, "I think you'll see an increase in people like me" (204). As he observes Frank with fascinated horror – a Marlow to his client's Kurtz – Kenji shifts roles from guide to the one being guided. "I can't deny that my body and mind were being dragged into unfamiliar territory," he admits late in the novel; "I felt like I was listening to the tales of a guide in some unexplored country" (202). The foreign visitor reveals the heart of darkness hidden beneath the bright neon lights of metropolitan Tokyo.

Set entirely within a few Tokyo neighborhoods, *In the Miso Soup* is a multinational narrative in a "glocalized" mode. It is equally possible, however, for a multinational work to take a delocalized approach, multiplying border crossings to the vanishing point – a perspective comically expressed in the title of a 1969 film, *If It's Tuesday, This Must Be Belgium*. A striking fictional treatment of multinational blurring is Christine Brooke-Rose's novel *Between*. Its unnamed heroine works as a simultaneous translator, and she spends much of her time in the air, flying from one conference to another. She is always between countries, relationships, and identities, a fact the novel embodies linguistically: the verb "to be" never appears in the book in any form, and the heroine never uses the pronoun "I."

In contrast to a purely delocalized work by Kafka or Beckett, *Between* includes scenes in specific countries, including England, France, Spain, Italy, Germany, Poland, Slovenia, Greece, Turkey, and the United States. Yet the pace of the heroine's multinational life is such that actions repeat themselves again and again, and one hotel room merges into another:

> At any minute now some bright or elderly or sour no young and buxom chambermaid in black and white will come in with a breakfast-tray, put it down on the table in the dark and draw back the curtains unless open the shutters and say Buenos días, Morgen or kalimera who knows, it all depends where the sleeping has occurred out of what dream shaken up with non merci nein danke no thank you in a long-lost terror of someone offering etwas anderes, not ordered. (Brooke-Rose 396)

Christine Brooke-Rose goes far beyond Kipling or even Rushdie in her use of foreign languages. Instead of an admixture of a single foreign language such as Hindi, her text presents a kaleidoscope of phrases and snatches of conversation in more than a dozen languages. Often, as above, a string of terms all reflect a single archetypal situation and so can serve as mutual translations. At other times, though, the heroine recalls snatches of conversation in other languages, most often French or German. When she began working as an interpreter just after the end of the Second World War, her first boss (and soon lover) was a German – ironically named Siegfried – working with the victorious Allies on denazification and the resettlement of refugees, and from then on she moved in multilingual circles.

The blizzard of languages brings the heroine's disorientation home to the reader, but the novel has a firm linguistic base in English, and gradually we become acclimated to this vertiginous world. We begin to take pleasure in the often hilarious slippage from one language to another – in Spain *la leche* turns lecherous, while an absent lover's loins are *loin* in France – as our heroine proceeds from the Congress of Acupuncturists to the Conference of Gnostics. As she dozes during her incessant airplane flights, multilingual memories swirl around in her consciousness, as when a Slovenian foreign minister's speech in French merges into a Dutch airline's instructions for inflating a life vest, and then morphs into a remembered elevator ride in Germany – or France? Italy? – in search of a toilet:

> — Mesdames messieurs. Aujourd'hui nous allons discuter la problème de la communication, du point de vue which reveals een bewusteloos persoon blowing hot air into the mouthpiece all enclosed in a glass booth going down, after having pulled red toggle. . . . But R turns out to mean Restaurant in studded black plastic cushioned walls not Rez-de-chaussée at all.
>
> Kein Eintritt. Privat. Que cherchez-vous madame? Ah, au fond à gauche, in fondo a sinistra geradeaus dann links according to the theme the time the place with a flared-skirted figurine on the door. Or a high-heeled shoe perhaps as opposed to a flat foot. (409–10)

Brooke-Rose's heroine struggles to locate herself within a consumerist world. An ad for an Italian detergent prompts her to a skeptical reflection: "Lava ancora più bianco! Gut-gut. Più bianco than what? We live in an age of transition, perpetually between white and whiter than white. Very tiring. Zoom" (419). As her travels continue, gradually she sorts out her memories of growing up caught between combatant nations in war-torn Europe, and she finally disentangles herself from a series of problematic men. Her continually in-between state is often confusing, but it enables her to escape the fixed female roles (office girl, wife, mistress) that the men in her life keep expecting her to play, even as she transcends the limitations of any single national identity.

Contemporary novels treat globalization as a powerful force with ambiguous effects. Globalization blurs national borders and unsettles moral codes, even as repressed conflicts continue to well up in uncanny ways. Yet it fosters freedom and self-invention, dissolving provincialisms and shaking up all routines. In the closing pages of *Between*, Brooke-Rose's heroine has achieved a new contentment as a self-sufficient or "alleinstehende Frau" (565) – literally, a "free-standing woman," in contrast to her unstable previous mixture of dependency and free-floating anxiety. Abandoning the constant life of mass transit by air, she buys a compact French car for journeys on her own. She makes sure to pack her British passport and a Turkish phrasebook, for her first destination will be Istanbul, here as often an emblem of life in-between (564). As she leaves the book's final conference, she hears the global babble fading away behind her, "as the members of the Congress on Tradition and Innovation unless perhaps The Role of the Writer in the Modern World burble on" (574).

*

Christine Brooke-Rose's resilient heroine can model for us the adaptive process of coming to terms with the expansive landscape of the world's languages, literatures, and cultures. In writing this book, I have sought to create a road map for explorations into our ever-widening literary world. The Epilogue will offer some initial directions for routes to consider, but whatever your choice of pathways – courses, anthologies, clusters of writers in whichever periods and regions most attract you – the issues raised in the preceding chapters can help you get your bearings and make sense of your discoveries. I will have succeeded in my endeavor if you are now well launched on your way, ready to carry on with the endless challenge and pleasure of world literature: to read, and read, and read still more.

Epilogue

Going Farther

And so, what to read?

The preceding chapters have offered guidance on major issues we face in reading world literature, and the examples discussed can suggest modes of entry into these works and into many more. Yet there remains the large question of how to go about choosing what to read, among the innumerable works written around the world during the past five thousand years. Serendipity always has a valuable role, of course: great finds can result from a friend's recommendation, or an intriguing book review, or an hour's browsing in a bookstore. Yet purely random reading – as when the Autodidact in Jean-Paul Sartre's novel *La Nausée* plows through the library shelves in alphabetical order – will rapidly become bewildering. A fuller exploration of world literature will benefit from some more organized approach.

One good way to proceed is to take hints from a favorite author. We will probably love works that have been important to a writer we love. Laurence Sterne speaks in *Tristram Shandy* of "my dear Rabelais, and dearer Cervantes" (169), and anyone who has been captivated by Sterne's self-reflexive hijinks and moved by the underlying melancholy of Uncle Toby's war-wounded life will be primed to enjoy *Gargantua and Pantagruel* and *Don Quixote*. Tracing lines of influence and adaptation can also provide a coherent way to explore a broad literary movement or tradition. Primo Levi or James Joyce may lead us back to Dante, and Dante to Virgil, Virgil to Homer. The very title of Chinua Achebe's *Things Fall Apart* announces a commonality of theme and feeling between the Nigerian novelist and the anticolonial Irish poet; Achebe underlines the link by setting the relevant lines of Yeats's "The Second Coming" as the epigraph to his book.

Quite apart from direct literary references, if you have been struck by a writer from a given time and place, you will likely want to see if there are more where that one came from. Sometimes a masterpiece stands almost alone in its time and place, but more often a great writer is the product of a vibrant literary culture. Anyone drawn to Sophocles will be deeply moved by Aeschylus and Euripides, and a lover of Du Fu's lyrics has a host of pleasures to explore in other Tang Dynasty poets such as Han Yu and Li Bo. Such further reading within a culture can also bring one's initial favorite into sharp relief, clarifying what is most distinctive about Sophocles or Du Fu as well as revealing what is broadly characteristic of their wider literary culture.

One convenient way to gain a broader sense of possibilities is to read around in collections and anthologies, which can give a manageable overview of a major tradition and a basis for further exploration thereafter. The six-volume survey anthologies of world literature published by Norton (Lawall et al.), Bedford (Davis et al.) and Longman (Damrosch et al.) each contains a wealth of judiciously selected works. More focused anthologies present examples of a genre; particularly useful are several excellent poetry anthologies, including Washburn, Major, and Fadiman's *World Poetry*, J. D. McClatchy's *The Vintage Book of Contemporary World Poetry*, and Jeffrey Paine's *The Poetry of Our World*. Other collections have a regional focus, such as Bassam Frangieh's *Anthology of Arabic Literature, Culture, and Thought from Pre-Islamic Times to the Present*, Robert Irwin's *Night and Horses and the Desert: An Anthology of Classical Arabic Literature*, Donald Keene's *Anthology of Japanese Literature from the Earliest Era to the Mid-Nineteenth Century*, Haruo Shirane's *Early Modern Japanese Literature: An Anthology, 1600–1900*, and Stephen Owen's *An Anthology of Chinese Literature: Beginnings to 1911*. Even the early literatures of the ancient Near East, formerly widely dispersed in specialized publications, can now be read in excellent translations in paperback editions: W. K. Simpson's *The Literature of Ancient Egypt*, Benjamin Foster's *Before the Muses: An Anthology of Akkadian Literature*, and Stephanie Dalley's *Myths from Mesopotamia*. Beyond anthologies, the Penguin Classics series gives an unparalleled range of works from around the world, while the Heinemann African Writers Series includes more than sixty writers from some two dozen African countries.

Heinemann's website provides biographies for their authors, and the Longman, Norton, and Bedford anthologies also have websites that offer a great deal of contextual information, readily accessed through the publishers' websites. An ambitious website devoted to contemporary literature is *Words without Borders: The Online Magazine for International Literature.* The print journal *World Literature Today* is also an excellent place to become acquainted with new writers from around the world.

A growing number of colleges and universities offer courses in world literature. Often a one-semester or year-long survey course provides an initial introduction, a gateway to a range of comparative and world literature courses thereafter. Survey courses can be organized in a variety of ways, and sometimes different instructors at the same school will employ very different approaches. A survey course can proceed chronologically, often also focusing in turn on several "major cultures" in the premodern period and then taking a global view for more recent literature; other courses are organized by genre or by theme. Some courses pair premodern and modern works, such as Ovid's *Metamorphoses* and Kafka's *Metamorphosis*. Within any of these approaches, a course can focus on a few works read at length or can present briefer selections from a greater range of writers. Where more than one of these options is available, it is worth looking into them to see which best suits your needs and interests.

Anyone wishing to explore ways to organize a world literature course will find very useful discussions by three dozen teachers in Damrosch (ed.), *Teaching World Literature*, and there are also several valuable earlier collections: Barbara Stoler Miller's *Masterworks of Asian Literature in Comparative Perspective: A Guide for Teaching*, Sarah Lawall's *Reading World Literature*, and Michael Thomas Carroll's *No Small World: Visions and Revisions of World Literature.* The Modern Language Association (MLA) also publishes many volumes devoted to teaching individual works or clusters of works in their series "Approaches to Teaching World Literature." The MLA also has several other relevant series: Options for Teaching; Texts and Translations; Teaching Languages, Literatures, and Cultures; and World Literatures Reimagined.

Students as well as teachers may want to delve into scholarly discussions of world literature. A good starting-point is John Pizer, *The Idea of World Literature*, which traces the heritage of Goethe's concept of *Weltliteratur* in German intellectual history and in American classrooms. A lively, sometimes polemical series of essays can be found in Christopher Prendergast (ed.), *Debating World Literature*, several of whose contributors respond to Pascale Casanova's study *The World Republic of Letters*. Another influential methodological study is Franco Moretti's *Graphs, Maps, and Trees: Abstract Models for a Literary History*, while issues of the production and circulation of world literature are explored in Damrosch, *What is World Literature?*

Those wishing to follow up on the crucial issue of translation can consult a range of important contributions to translation studies. The best place to start is with Lawrence Venuti's capacious collection of classic essays, *The Translation Studies Reader*. Mona Baker's *Routledge Encyclopedia of Translation Studies* is an excellent reference work, while Susan Bassnett-McGuire's *Translation Studies* gives an overview of the history of the field. Some valuable studies of different aspects of translation are: Susan Bassnett and Harish Trivedi (eds.) *Post-Colonial Translation: Theory and Practice*; Sandra Bermann and Michael Wood (eds.) *Nation, Language, and the Ethics of Translation*; Sherry Simon, *Gender in Translation*; Maria Tymoczko and Edwin Gentzler (eds.), *Translation and Power*; and Lawrence Venuti, *The Scandals of Translation: Towards an Ethics of Difference*.

Several important recent books address the history and ongoing development of Comparative Literature, the field most centrally concerned with world literature. Recent works of note include Emily Apter, *The Translation Zone: A New Comparative Literature*, Gayatri Chakravorty Spivak, *Death of a Discipline*, and Natalie Melas, *All the Difference in the World*. Collections of classic essays in the field can be found in Damrosch, Melas, and Buthelezi (eds.), *The Text and the World: A Comparative Literature Sourcebook*, and in Hans-Joachim Schultz and Phillip H. Rhein (eds.), *Comparative Literature: The Early Years*.

As much as there is to read, there are other ways to deepen our understanding of world literature as well. One prime method is to get to know other art forms from the cultures whose literature we read. The major anthologies now come with many illustrations and with accompanying audio CDs; their companion websites offer many more artworks and audio links. Then there are the major benefits to be gained by studying works in the original language whenever possible. As valuable as translations are, they achieve their best results if they inspire readers to go and learn the language. It can take a great deal of time to achieve near-native fluency, but even an intermediate knowledge of a language is enormously liberating, freeing us from complete dependency on translations and allowing us entry into the many pleasures of a writer's style that can only be glimpsed in translation. Ideally, every serious reader of world literature should know at least two foreign languages, one from one's home region and one from a very different part of the world and an unrelated language family. It is fascinating to discover how very differently languages can organize such basic categories as time and gender, and such linguistic differences can have profound literary effects. Further language study beyond those two will be all the better.

Finally, reading world literature should stimulate us to get out into the world. Though no literary work is a direct mirror of its society, all writers come out of a culture and respond to it in many ways, even if they choose to respond by fleeing their home environment. The more we know about the culture of origin – its peoples and daily customs, its landscape, its architecture, its flowers and birdsongs – the more fully we can understand the transformations that a writer has wrought. Spending time attentively abroad can tell us a good deal about Dostoevsky's St. Petersburg or Murasaki Shibiku's Kyoto, despite all the changes since those authors' time. Studying abroad can tell us far more. Study abroad is particularly valuable in programs and places that foster full immersion in the culture, rather than merely providing a bubble of visiting students or expatriates. We can then return home with deepened understanding and new possibilities for enjoyment, as we continue reading our way into the literary legacies of the past and the multiple worlds opening out before us today.

Bibliography

Achebe, Chinua. "An Image of Africa: Racism in Conrad's *Heart of Darkness*." *The Massachusetts Review* 18:4 (1977), 782–94.

_____. *Things Fall Apart*. London: Penguin, 2001.

Ali, Tariq. "Literature and Market Realism." *New Left Review* 199 (1993), 140–5.

Apter, Emily. *The Translation Zone: A New Comparative Literature*. Princeton: Princeton University Press, 2005.

Apuleius. *Metamorphoses*, ed. and tr. J. Arthur Hanson. Loeb Classical Library 44. Cambridge, MA and London: Harvard University Press. 2 vols., 1989.

Aristophanes. *Lysistrata*. In *Four Comedies*, tr. Dudley Fitts. New York: Harcourt, Brace & World, 1959, 1–68.

_____. *Lysistrata*, tr. Douglass Parker. New York: New American Library, 1964.

_____. *Lysistrata*, tr. Jeffrey Henderson. Newburyport, MA: Focus Publishing, 1988.

_____. *Lysistrata*. In *The Complete Plays*, tr. Paul Roche. New York: New American Library, 2005, 415–78.

Aristotle. *The Poetics of Aristotle*, tr. Preston H. Epps. Chapel Hill: University of North Carolina Press, 1975.

Baker, Mona. *The Routledge Encyclopedia of Translation Studies*. London and New York: Routledge, 2001.

Baraka, Amiri. *The System of Dante's Hell*. In *Three Books by Imamu Amiri Baraka (LeRoi Jones)*. New York: Grove Press, 1967, 5–154.

Bassnett, Susan, and Harish Trivedi, eds. *Post-Colonial Translation: Theory and Practice*. London: Routledge, 1999.

Bassnett-McGuire, Susan. *Translation Studies*. London and New York: Methuen, 1980.

Behn, Aphra. *Oroonoko, or The Royal Slave: A True History*, ed. Joanna Lipking. New York: W. W. Norton, 1997.

Benjamin, Walter. "The Task of the Translator." In *Illuminations*, ed. Hannah Arendt, tr. Harry Zohn. New York: Schocken, 1969, 69–82. Repr. in Venuti, *The Translation Studies Reader*, 2d ed., 75–85.

Bermann, Sandra, and Michael Wood, eds. *Nation, Language, and the Ethics of Translation.* Princeton: Princeton University Press, 2005.

Bierhorst, John, ed. and tr. *Cantares Mexicanos: Songs of the Aztecs.* Stanford: Stanford University Press, 1985.

Bloom, Harold. *The Western Canon: The Books and School of the Ages.* New York: Riverhead, 1994.

Borges, Jorge Luis. *Collected Fictions,* tr. Andrew Hurley. New York: Viking, 1998.

____. *Selected Non-Fictions,* tr. Eliot Weinberger, Esther Allen, and Suzanne Jill Levine. New York: Viking, 1999, Penguin, 2000.

Brooke-Rose, Christine. *Between.* In *The Christine Brooke-Rose Omnibus: Four Novels.* Manchester and New York: Carcanet, 1986, 391–575.

Burton, Richard F., ed. and tr. *A Plain and Literal Translation of the Arabian Nights Entertainment, Now Entitled the Book of the Thousand Nights and a Night.* Benares (Stoke Newington), 10 vols., 1885.

____. *Supplemental Nights to the Book of the Thousand Nights and a Night.* Benares (Stoke Newington), 6 vols., 1886–8.

Calvino, Italo. *Invisible Cities,* tr. William Weaver. San Diego: Harcourt, Brace, 1972.

____. "Presentazione." *Le città invisibili.* Milan: Mondadori, 1993, v–xi.

Carroll, Lewis. *The Annotated Snark,* ed. Martin Gardner. New York: Bramhall House, 1962.

Carroll, Michael Thomas, ed. *No Small World: Visions and Revisions of World Literature.* Urbana, IL: National Council of Teachers of English, 1996.

Casanova, Pascale. *La République mondiale des lettres.* Paris: Editions du Seuil, 1999. *The World Republic of Letters,* tr. M. B. DeBevoise. Cambridge, MA and London: Harvard University Press, 2004.

Caws, Mary Ann, et al., eds. *The HarperCollins World Reader.* New York: HarperCollins, 1994.

Chikamatsu Mon'zaemon. *Love Suicides at Amijima.* In *Major Plays of Chikamatsu,* tr. Donald Keene. New York: Columbia University Press, 1990.

Conrad, Joseph. *Heart of Darkness,* ed. Ross C. Murfin. Boston: Bedford/St. Martin's. 2d ed., 1996.

Cortázar, Julio. *Rayuela,* ed. Andrés Amorós. Buenos Aires: Catedra, 3rd ed., 1986. *Hopscotch,* tr. Gregory Rabassa. New York: Pantheon, 1966.

Dalley, Stephanie. *Myths from Mesopotamia.* London and New York: Oxford, 1989.

Damrosch, David. *What Is World Literature?* Princeton: Princeton University Press, 2003.

____, David L. Pike, et al., eds. *The Longman Anthology of World Literature.* New York: Pearson Longman, 6 vols., 2004.

____, ed. *Teaching World Literature.* New York: Modern Language Association, 2009.

____, Natalie Melas, and Mbongiseni Buthelezi, eds. *The Text and the World: A Comparative Literature Sourcebook.* Princeton: Princeton University Press, 2009.

Darbishire, Helen, ed. *Journals of Dorothy Wordsworth*. London: Oxford University Press, 1958.

Davis, Paul, et al., eds. *The Bedford Anthology of World Literature*. Boston: Bedford/ St. Martin's, 6 vols., 2003.

Dawood, N. J., tr. *Tales from The Thousand and One Nights*. Harmondsworth: Penguin, rev. ed., 1973.

Dryden, John. Preface to Ovid's *Epistles*. In Venuti, *The Translation Studies Reader*, 2d ed., 38–42.

Ellmann, Richard. *James Joyce*. New York: Oxford, rev. ed., 1982.

Foster, Benjamin. *Before the Muses: An Anthology of Akkadian Literature*. Bethesda, MD: CDL Press, 2005.

Frangieh, Bassam K. *Anthology of Arabic Literature, Culture, and Thought from Pre-Islamic Times to the Present*. New Haven: Yale University Press, 2005.

Genesis. In *The New Oxford Annotated Bible, with the Apocrypha*. Revised Standard Version. New York: Oxford University Press, 1977, 1–66.

George, Andrew, ed. and tr. *The Epic of Gilgamesh: A New Translation*. London: Penguin, 1999.

Graham, A. C., ed. and tr. *Poems of the Late T'ang*. Harmondsworth: Penguin, 1965.

Haddawy, Husein, ed. and tr. *The Arabian Nights*. New York and London: Norton, 1990.

_____. *The Arabian Nights II: Sindbad and Other Popular Stories*. New York and London: Norton, 1995.

Hartley, L. P. *The Go-Between*. London: Hamilton, 1953.

Homer, *The Iliad*, tr. Robert Fagles. New York: Viking, 1990.

_____. *The Odyssey*, tr. Robert Fagles. New York: Viking, 1996.

Hutner, Heidi, ed. *Rereading Aphra Behn: History, Theory, and Criticism*. Charlottesville: University Press of Virginia, 1993.

Ingalls, Daniel H. H. et al., ed. and tr. *The Dhvanyāloka of Anandavardhana with the Locana of Abhinavagupta*. Cambridge, MA: Harvard University Press, 1990.

Irwin, Robert. *Night and Horses and the Desert: An Anthology of Classical Arabic Literature*. New York: Anchor, 2002.

Johnson, John William, ed. and tr. *The Epic of Son-Jara: A West African Tradition*. Text by Fa-Digi Sisòkò. Bloomington: Indiana University Press, 1992.

Joyce, James. *Ulysses*, ed. Hans Walter Gabler. New York: Random House, 1986.

Kalidasa. *Śakuntalā and the Ring of Recollection*, tr. Barbara Stoler Miller. In *Theater of Memory: The Plays of Kālidāsa*, ed. Barbara Stoler Miller et al. New York: Columbia University Press, 1984.

Keats, John. *Keats*, ed. Howard Moss. New York: Dell, 1959.

Keene, Donald. *Anthology of Japanese Literature from the Earliest Era to the Mid-Nineteenth Century*. New York: Grove Press, 1955.

Kipling, Rudyard. *Departmental Ditties*. In *The Works of Kipling*. Roslyn, New York: Black, n.d., 1–14.

_____. *Kim*. New York: Dell, 1979.

Lane, Edward William, tr. *Stories from The Thousand and One Nights*. Rev. by Stanley Lane-Poole. The Harvard Classics. New York: Collier, 1937.

Lawall, Sarah, ed. *Reading World Literature: Theory, History, Practice*. Austin: University of Texas Press, 1994.

_____, et al., eds. *The Norton Anthology of World Literature*. New York: W. W. Norton, 6 vols., 2003.

Lichtheim, Miriam. *Ancient Egyptian Literature: A Book of Readings*. Berkeley: University of California Press, 3 vols., 1973–80.

Lukács, Georg. *Theory of the Novel: A Historico-philosophical Essay on the Forms of Great Epic Literature*, tr. Anna Bostock. Cambridge, MA: MIT Press, 1973.

MacLeish, Archibald. "Ars Poetica." In Robert Hass et al., eds., *American Poetry: The Twentieth Century*. New York: Library of America, 1:846–7.

McClatchy, J. D., ed. *The Vintage Book of Contemporary World Poetry*. New York: Vintage, 1996.

Melas, Natalie. *All the Difference in the World: Postcoloniality and the Ends of Comparison*. Stanford: Stanford University Press, 2007.

Miller, Barbara Stoler, ed. *Masterworks of Asian Literature in Comparative Perspective: A Guide for Teaching*. Armonk, New York and London: M. E. Sharpe, 1994.

Milton, John. *Paradise Lost*, ed. Merritt Y. Hughes. Indianapolis: Bobbs-Merrill, 1962.

Molière, Jean-Baptiste Poquelin. *The Miser and Other Plays*, tr. John Wood. Baltimore: Penguin, 1953.

Moretti, Franco. *Graphs, Maps, and Trees: Abstract Models for a Literary History*. London and New York: Verso, 2005.

Murakami, Ryu. *In the Miso Soup*, tr. Ralph McCarthy. New York: Penguin, 2003.

Murasaki Shikibu. *The Tale of Genji*, tr. Royall Tyler. New York: Viking, 2 vols., 2001.

Ortega y Gasset, José. "La Miseria y el esplendor de la traducción," tr. Elizabeth Gamble Miller as "The Misery and the Splendor of Translation." In Venuti, *The Translation Studies Reader*, 1st ed., 49–63.

Owen, Stephen. *Traditional Chinese Poetry and Poetics: Omen of the World*. Madison: University of Wisconsin Press, 1985.

_____, ed. *An Anthology of Chinese Literature: Beginnings to 1911*. New York: W. W. Norton, 1997.

Paine, Jeffrey, ed. *The Poetry of Our World: An International Anthology of Contemporary Poetry*. New York: Harper Perennial, 2001.

Pamuk, Orhan. *The Black Book*, tr. Maureen Freely. New York: Vintage, 2006.

_____. *My Name Is Red*, tr. Erdağ M. Göknar. New York: Vintage, 2001.

_____. *Other Colors: Essays and a Story*, tr. Maureen Freely. New York: Knopf, 2007.

Pindar. *Pindar's Victory Songs*, tr. Frank J. Nisetsch. Baltimore: Johns Hopkins University Press, 1980.

Pizarnik, Alejandra, *Obras completas: poesía y prosa*, ed. Cristina Piña. Buenos Aires: Corregidor, 1994.

Pizer, John. *The Idea of World Literature*. Baton Rouge: Louisiana State University Press, 2006.

Polo, Marco. *The Travels*, tr. Ronald Latham. Harmondsworth: Penguin, 1958.

Prendergast, Christopher, ed. *Debating World Literature*. London and New York: Verso, 2004.

Pritchard, James B. *Ancient Near Eastern Texts Relating to the Old Testament*. Princeton: Princeton University Press, 3rd ed., 1969.

Quiller-Couch, Arthur. *The Oxford Book of English Verse 1250–1900*. Oxford: Clarendon Press, 1919.

Ronsard, Pierre de. *Oeuvres complètes*, ed. M. Prosper Blanchemain. Paris: Jannet, 8 vols., 1857–67.

Rushdie, Salman. *East, West*. London: Vintage, 1995.

Schultz, Hans-Joachim, and Phillip H. Rhein, eds. *Comparative Literature: The Early Years*. Chapel Hill: University of North Carolina Press, 1973.

Seferis, George. *Collected Poems (1924–1955)*, tr. Edmund Keeley and Philip Sherrard. Princeton: Princeton University Press, 1971, 46–8.

Shakespeare, William. *The Tempest*, ed. Northrop Frye. Baltimore: Penguin, 1970.

Shirane, Haruo, ed. *Early Modern Japanese Literature: An Anthology, 1600–1900*. New York: Columbia University Press, 2004.

Sidney, Sir Phillip. *The Defense of Poesy*. In Michael Payne and John Hunter, eds., *Renaissance Literature: An Anthology*. Oxford: Blackwell, 2003, 501–26.

Simon, Sherry. *Gender in Translation: Cultural Identity and the Politics of Transmission*. London and New York: Routledge, 1996.

Simpson, William Kelly, ed. *The Literature of Ancient Egypt: An Anthology of Stories, Instructions, Stelae, Autobiographies, and Poetry*. New Haven: Yale University Press, 3rd ed., 2003.

Song of Songs (The Song of Solomon). In *The New Oxford Annotated Bible, with the Apocrypha*. Revised Standard Version. New York: Oxford University Press, 1977, 815–21.

Sophocles. *Oedipus the King*, tr. David Grene. Chicago: University of Chicago Press, 1942.

Soyinka, Wole. *Death and the King's Horseman*, ed. Simon Gikandi. New York: W. W. Norton, 2003.

Spivak, Gayatri Chakravorty. *Death of a Discipline*. New York: Columbia University Press, 2003.

Sterne, Laurence. *The Life and Opinions of Tristram Shandy*. New York: Modern Library, n.d.

"Šulgi N." Electronic Text Corpus of Sumerian Literature (www.etcsl.orient.ox.ac.uk), text 2.4.2.02.

Swift, Jonathan. *Gulliver's Travels*, ed. Robert A. Greenberg. New York: W. W. Norton, 1970.

Tibullus. *Elegies*. In *Catullus, Tibullus, and Pervigilium Veneris*, ed. G. P. Goolde. Loeb Classical Library. Cambridge, MA: Harvard University Press, 2d ed., 1988.

Tymoczko, Maria, and Edwin Gentzler, eds. *Translation and Power*. Amherst: University of Massachusetts Press, 2002.

Venuti, Lawrence. *The Scandals of Translation: Towards an Ethics of Difference*. London and New York: Routledge, 1998.

_____, ed. *The Translation Studies Reader*. New York and London: Routledge, 2000. Rev. ed., 2004.

Virgil. *Eclogues, Georgics, Aeneid, the Minor Poems*, ed. and tr. H. R. Fairclough. Loeb Classical Library. Cambridge, MA: Harvard University Press, 2 vols., 1978.

_____. *The Aeneid*, tr. Robert Fitzgerald. New York: Random House, 1983.

Voltaire, François-Marie Arouet de. *Candid: or, All for the Best*. London: Printed for J. Nourse, 1759.

_____. *Candide*. Anonymous Victorian-era translation. Repr. in *The Complete Romances of Voltaire*, ed. G. W. B. New York: Walter J. Black, 1927, 121–85.

_____. *Candide ou l'optimisme*. In *Romans et contes*, ed. René Pomeau. Paris: Garnier, 1966, 179–259.

_____. *Candide, or Optimism*, tr. Robert M. Adams. New York: W. W. Norton, 2d ed., 1991. Repr. in Sarah Lawall et al., eds., *The Norton Anthology of World Literature*. New York: W. W. Norton. 2d ed., 2002, vol. D: 520–80.

_____. *Candide, or Optimism*, tr. Daniel Gordon. Boston: Bedford / St. Martin's, 1998. Repr. in Davis et al., eds., *The Bedford Anthology of World Literature*, 2003, vol. 4: 275–338.

Walcott, Derek. *Omeros*. New York: Farrar, Straus, and Giroux, 1990.

Washburn, Katharine, John S. Major, and Clifton Fadiman, eds. *World Poetry: An Anthology of Verse from Antiquity to Our Time*. New York: W. W. Norton, 1998.

West, M. L. *The East Face of Helicon: West Asiatic Elements in Greek Poetry and Myth*. Oxford: Clarendon Press, 1997.

Wisdom of Solomon, The. In *The Apocrypha*. Revised Standard Version. New York: Oxford University Press, 1977, 102–27.

Words without Borders: The Online Magazine for International Literature. www.wordswithoutborders.org.

Wordsworth, William. *The Poems of William Wordsworth*, ed. Nowel Charles Smith. London: Methuen, 3 vols., 1908.

Index